FULL DRAW

Michael Birky

The Outdoorsman's Guide to a Life of Focus and Faith

Copyright © 2025 KnoWhere Outdoors, LLC

All rights reserved.

No part of this publication may be reproduced, stored in a retrieval system, or transmitted in any form or by any means—electronic, mechanical, photocopying, recording, or otherwise—without the prior written permission of the publisher, except in the case of brief quotations used in articles or reviews.

ISBN: 979-8-9989017-1-3

Printed in United States of America

First Edition

Published by KnoWhere Outdoors, LLC

Disclaimer:

This devotional is for inspirational and educational purposes only and is not intended as a substitute for professional advice or counseling. The views expressed are those of the author and are based on personal experiences and biblical interpretation. Always seek guidance from trusted mentors, pastors, and your personal study of Scripture.

Some names and identifying details have been changed to protect the privacy of individuals.

To my family, thank you for loving me and always supporting the man I strive to be.

To my hunting buddies, past and present, thanks for the memories and the laughs.

To every outdoorsman picking up this devotional, may you walk with purpose and live each day with faith-filled focus.

WORDS OF ENCOURAGEMENT

" Whether you're sitting in a blind or standing in a river casting your line in the water, you are living with a clear aim for what you're after. What you hold in your hands will help any outdoorsman live their one and only life with faith, loyalty and a willingness to sacrifice like Christ did. Michael Birky has given us an absolute gift with this devotional to help you live on mission, with obedience and accuracy towards what matters most. If your target is growing closer to Christ and deepening your faith, then this book is going to do wonders for your soul.

STEVE CARTER
*LEAD PASTOR OF CHRIST CHURCH OF OAK BROOK AND THE BESTSELLING AUTHOR OF **THE THING BENEATH THE THING***

" *Full Draw* is such a good mix of autobiography and spiritual outfitting. It's a strong reminder that discipline and faithfulness matter on the hunt, in our work, in our homes, and in our daily walk with Jesus. This devotional can guide any man who wants to live with purpose and pass on a legacy rooted in faith.

DAVID GRIFFITH
HUSBAND, FATHER, OUTDOORSMAN, AND FOLLOWER OF CHRIST

CONTENTS

INTRODUCTION: PREPARING FOR THE HUNT OF A LIFETIME... 9

PRE-SEASON
Day 1: Strategic Preparation.. 14
Day 2: Scouting the Terrain... 19
Day 3: Sighting In.. 23
Day 4: Planting with Purpose... 27
Day 5: The Perfect Setup.. 31
Day 6: Trust Built on Boundaries..................................... 36
Day 7: Fireside Fellowship... 40

MID-SEASON
Day 8: The Morning Jitters... 46
Day 9: The Power of Stillness... 50
Day 10: Scent Control... 54
Day 11: Faith Beyond What's Seen.................................. 58
Day 12: Beware the Bear... 62
Day 13: Eyes on the Prize.. 66
Day 14: Weathering the Storm.. 70
Day 15: Aiming for Grace... 75
Day 16: Entrusted, Not Owned.. 80
Day 17: Sometimes We Stumble...................................... 84

LATE-SEASON
Day 18: More Than The Rut.. 92
Day 19: Worth The Wait... 96
Day 20: The Weight of the Moment.................................. 100
Day 21: One Step At A Time (Part 1)................................ 104
Day 22: One Step At A Time (Part 2)................................ 108
Day 23: Just A Mount... 112
Day 24: Consequences in the Compromise....................... 116

POST-SEASON
Day 25: Looking Back to Move Forward............................ 122
Day 26: The Source of It All... 126
Day 27: Quality Time, Lasting Impact............................... 132
Day 28: A Shed of Evidence... 135
Day 29: Passing It On... 139
Day 30: Rooted in Gratitude... 144
Day 31: A Legacy That Lasts.. 148

EPILOGUE.. 152
ACKNOWLEDGMENTS... 153

INTRODUCTION:
PREPARING FOR THE HUNT OF A LIFETIME

Welcome to *Full Draw*, a space where hunting, faith, and everyday life come together with clarity and intention. Whether you are deep in the woods, out on the water, or managing everyday life, one truth remains clear. Success never happens by chance. Every seasoned outdoorsman knows that success, whether it's bagging a buck, landing a trophy bass, or simply enjoying the beauty of creation, comes through preparation, patience, and a commitment to doing things the right way. The same is true for our spiritual lives. Without intentional preparation and focus, we risk being caught off guard when life's challenges come our way.

This devotional is designed to equip you with the tools you need to stay sharp, grounded, and spiritually ready—so when the moment of truth arrives, you'll be prepared to face whatever lies ahead with faith and confidence. Over the next 31 days, you'll engage with daily devotionals that connect your passion for the outdoors with timeless biblical truths. Each day is broken into five sections, giving you practical and spiritual insights to apply both in the field and in life.

As you work through these devotionals, you'll notice that some themes such as focus, patience, perseverance, and trust are repeated in different ways. That's intentional. Just as consistent practice is essential for becoming a better outdoorsman, revisiting these core principles strengthens your faith and sharpens your spiritual focus. These core principles are essential, but they're only part of the journey. As you dive deeper, you'll also encounter themes that challenge and equip you spiritually—such as living with intentionality, growing through trials, and leaving a legacy of faith.

These are just some of the powerful themes you'll explore, each one designed to shape a life that honors God both in the outdoors and beyond.

Here's what you can expect:

SCRIPTURE

Each day begins with a passage of Scripture. The Bible is our foundation and guide—just as any good outdoorsman relies on their GPS to navigate the terrain. This Scripture will set the tone for the day and give you a spiritual framework to reflect on.

THE TARGET

The Target section follows the Scripture reading and establishes the key focus for the day. Think of it as setting your aim. It's where you zero in on the central message from the passage and prepare to apply it to your life. By reflecting on this focus, you're laying the groundwork for how you'll approach the challenges ahead. This section provides a clear objective that carries through the day's devotional, ultimately leading to the 1 M.O.A. section, where we focus on living out God's truth in practical ways (more on that in a bit).

ZEROED IN

This section blends real-life experiences—sometimes drawn from time spent outdoors, other times from everyday challenges—with a practical application. Some days, you'll read about moments in the field, while other days will explore insights drawn from life's ups and downs. Each story or reflection highlights an important spiritual principle, showing you how to apply God's truth in your own life. This section is designed to help you move beyond simply hearing the Word and instead prepare your heart to live it out.

1 M.O.A.

In the world of shooting, 1 M.O.A. (Minute of Angle) refers to the measurement of accuracy, ensuring that every shot is precise and on target. In this book, 1 M.O.A. takes on a deeper meaning—Mission, Obedience, and Accuracy. Just as a skilled marksman hones his focus and discipline to stay on target, we are called to live with intentionality and faithfulness in our spiritual walk.

Mission: What is the specific mission God is calling you to pursue? Every season begins with a clear goal, and in the same way, God gives each of us a unique purpose to fulfill. Recognizing that mission—whether it's leading your family, serving others, or growing in faith—helps you stay focused and intentional as you move forward.

Obedience: Are you walking in obedience to God's calling? Staying on the right path is essential for success, both in hunting and in faith. How can you align your steps with His plan and trust Him fully?

Accuracy: Are your actions reflecting the truth of God's Word? In shooting, precision determines success. Spiritually, living with accuracy means aligning your thoughts, words, and actions with God's commands so that your life hits the mark He's set before you.

PRAYER

At the end of each day's devotional, we'll close with a short prayer. These prayers are designed to help center your thoughts and align your heart with God's will. Think of them as a way to seal what you've read, bringing the lessons and reflections into your everyday life. Whether you say them aloud or reflect quietly, use them as a moment to invite God into your day and ask for His guidance as you pursue a life of focus and faith.

As you journey through this devotional, remember that each day is an opportunity to grow in focus, faith, and preparedness for whatever challenges may come. By committing to the principles in each chapter, you'll be better equipped to navigate life's uncertainties with confidence and trust in God's plan. As we embark on this journey together, trust that God will guide your steps and strengthen you for whatever lies ahead.

DAY 1
STRATEGIC PREPARATION

VERSE

Put on the full armor of God, so that you can take your stand against the devil's schemes.
Ephesians 6:11

THE TARGET

Ephesians 6:11 reminds us that we are in a battle, not against people, but against the unseen forces that try to pull us off course. The armor of God is not just a metaphor, it is something we need every single day. As you read and reflect, ask yourself if you are stepping into life prepared or hoping to get by without protection. The challenge is to suit up, stand strong, and refuse to face the day without the gear God has given you.

ZEROED IN

My wife and I live in a 3-bedroom house, and one of those bedrooms has become my hunting headquarters. It's my man cave, filled with gear, trophies, and memories of a hunter's life. The walk-in closet is a treasure trove of hunting clothes, shelves of carefully stacked gear, gun-cleaning supplies, and bows hanging on the wall. On the walls, there's a proud display of fish and deer mounts, all overseeing the room. It has a couch, a 65-inch TV, and my desk for those times when, unfortunately, work has to come first. My wife has graciously, though probably reluctantly, allowed me this space for now. We had our second baby girl, and she's in need of a bedroom.

   I'd like to think I'm an organized person, but I'm definitely a "pack the night before" type of guy. My approach to travel is, "If I forget something, I'll figure it out when I get there." When it comes to hunting, though, I try to be more deliberate. Even if I pack last minute, I've been thinking about what I need all off-season. I tend to overpack, ensuring I'm prepared for anything.

   Last deer season was no different. By the time gun season rolled around, I was in a good rhythm. I had my gear laid out on my couch, knew exactly how many layers I needed to stay warm without sweating, and had my timeline to the woods planned out to the minute. I'd calculated how long it would take to brush my teeth, load the truck, grab a breakfast sandwich, drive to the farm, and settle into my stand.

   One thing you should know about me is that I'm a big archery hunter. I've taken more deer with a bow than anything else, and until recently, I had never missed a deer. That streak ended on a 50-yard shot at an Oregon blacktail in the timber, but I still pride myself on my consistency with a bow. Gun season, on the other hand, has always been a different story. I've had many successful hunts, but I've forgotten choke tubes, insulated bibs, slugs—and once, even the gun itself. Honestly, at times I feel my gun season record is 2-15, and I'm on the clock for the first pick in the draft.

   As expected, opening day of the 2024 gun season didn't go entirely as planned. I followed my carefully mapped-out timeline and hit the road on time, but a few miles in, my truck's front-right tire gave me a low-pressure warning. I stopped to fill it with air, which put me behind schedule. To make up for lost time, I decided to skip grabbing breakfast. The rut was in full swing, and I didn't want to miss a minute of prime morning movement. About 45 minutes into the hour-and-fifteen-minute drive, I mentally ran through my gear list. My stomach dropped. I knew, without a doubt, that I'd left my hunter orange at home, on the couch in my office. In Indiana, a blaze orange hat is mandatory during gun season. Turning back wasn't an option; by the time I would make it home and return, the morning hunt would be close to over. My next thought was to just leave the gun in the truck and sit in the woods to observe. But that's when that nocturnal 12-point buck with a drop tine would stroll by at 30 yards broadside.

I pulled off at the next exit and searched for nearby stores that might actually sell a blaze orange hat at 5am. After ten minutes of checking, it became clear that nothing would be open until sunrise. Frustrated, I decided to head to the woods anyway and just enjoy the quiet morning. About 8 miles before the exit to the farm, my gas light came on. I stopped to fuel up and figured I'd check the convenience store for anything orange. To my surprise, they had a blaze orange beanie tucked away on a shelf. It wasn't exactly what I would've picked out—thick with a sparkly American flag on the front—but it would do the job. For $12, I couldn't pass it up.

I jumped back in the truck, and the "we're back, baby, we're so back!" was playing over and over in my head. I finally made it to the farm, about 15 minutes later than planned. After getting geared up, I managed to settle into my stand 45 minutes before legal shooting light. It wasn't the smoothest start, but I was there, ready to go, and thankful for the chance to be in the woods.

Ephesians 6:11 urges us to put on the full armor of God so we can stand strong against the enemy's plans. In the same way a hunter would never head into the woods unprepared, we are called to be spiritually ready for whatever the day brings. Preparation matters. In the field, that means packing wisely, checking your gear, and making sure everything is in working order. In life, it means making sure your heart and mind are aligned with God before stepping out into a world full of distractions, temptations, and spiritual resistance.

I've had more than one hunt thrown off by a lack of preparation—whether it was forgetting something simple like gloves or something more serious like my blaze orange. Those moments always drive home the point that success isn't just about skill or luck. It's about readiness, and spiritual readiness works the same way. You may not see the challenge coming, but when it does, you'll be thankful you were armored up through prayer, truth, and trust in God.

God's armor isn't physical gear, but it carries real power and purpose. In Ephesians 6:10–17, Paul describes each piece and its role in the believer's life. Truth keeps you grounded. Righteousness guards your heart. Peace gives you stability. Faith shields you from the lies and attacks that come your way. Salvation reminds you of your identity, and God's Word keeps you sharp and focused. Putting this on daily is not about ritual—it's about relationship and reliance.

Today, before you step into your responsibilities, take a moment to gear up. Invite God into your routine. Don't leave your spiritual armor on the shelf. A hunter doesn't prepare by accident, and neither should you. The battle is real. Show up ready.

1 M.O.A.

You wouldn't step into the woods without checking your gear. So why step into life without checking your heart? The enemy doesn't wait for a convenient moment to strike—he looks for when you're distracted, tired, or unarmed. Spiritual preparation isn't about going through the motions, it's about choosing to be alert, disciplined, and ready.

Mission: Cultivate a heart of readiness and preparation, both in your spiritual walk and in everyday life. Just as forgetting a small but important piece of hunting gear can impact a hunt, neglecting spiritual disciplines can leave you unprepared for the challenges ahead.

Obedience: Commit to starting each day with intentional preparation—whether through prayer, time in Scripture, or seeking wisdom from God. Identify one spiritual habit you need to strengthen and take an intentional step to develop it this week.

Accuracy: You'll recognize growth when you face unexpected challenges with confidence rather than panic. Instead of scrambling when difficulties arise, you'll be equipped with the peace and wisdom that come from consistently walking with God. A prepared heart leads to a steady faith.

PRAYER

Lord, thank You for providing everything I need to stay grounded and strong in this life. Help me to be intentional each day in putting on the full armor of God, so I can face the challenges ahead with confidence and strength. Equip me with Your Word, Your Spirit, and Your truth to guard my heart and mind. May I walk faithfully, ready for whatever comes my way, trusting in Your protection and guidance. In Jesus' name, Amen.

DAY 2
SCOUTING THE TERRAIN

VERSE

Trust in the Lord with all your heart and lean not on your own understanding; in all your ways submit to him, and he will make your paths straight.
Proverbs 3:5-6

THE TARGET

Navigating unfamiliar terrain can be tricky, especially when instincts alone lead you in the wrong direction. Proverbs 3:5-6 reminds us that true clarity and guidance come when we surrender our plans to God, trusting Him to chart our course. Scouting the terrain of life means seeking His direction, submitting your choices to His wisdom, and trusting that He will lead you along the right path—even if it doesn't immediately make sense.

ZEROED IN

How many times have you gone out hunting or fishing in a completely new place—a farm or lake you've never been to before—taking a chance on a spot you hoped would deliver? For me, there's always a mix of excitement and uncertainty in those moments. Nowadays, technology has made e-scouting a game changer. I can sit on my couch with my phone, pinpoint a few promising spots, and feel like I've got it figured out.

When I first started hunting, things weren't nearly as simple. There were no apps or GPS to guide me. I had to learn the land the hard way—putting in long, sweaty miles under the blazing Indiana sun. Nothing teaches you a property quite like walking the woods in ninety-degree heat, one step at a time. Fast forward to now, I have a lot more experience but honestly a lot less time. Between being a husband, a dad, and holding down a full-time job, those endless days of scouting are harder to come by. Still, I've built up enough knowledge that I feel confident looking at a map and identifying where I should set up—whether I'm hunting in the Midwest, reading water to find the best fishing spots, or working through the dense timber of the Pacific Northwest. But let's be real, do I actually know where I should go just from staring at a screen?

The answer is a big, resounding no. I can't think of one single time when I've hunted a new property and, on the first morning, sat in exactly the right spot. Sure, I might have been in the general area, but "close" doesn't fill tags. If you're reading this and thinking that sounds familiar, you're in good company. I think most of us have been there. Even with all the tools and tech in the world, there's no substitute for time, effort, and good old-fashioned trial and error.

Scouting is one of the most critical aspects of hunting. Any given year, I'm running four to six cell cams (which would honestly be 15 if those data plans weren't ridiculously expensive). I pay for subscriptions to hunting and fishing apps, invest in weather tools to track deer movement or fish activity, and try to squeeze in on-the-ground scouting whenever I can. It's a serious investment—not just financially but also in time. Time that could be spent with family or crossing off the never-ending list of home projects. And while there's always that guy we all know—the one who wakes up on opening morning, throws on his jeans and flannel shirt, strolls into the woods and tags a trophy 10-pointer by 9 a.m. For the rest of us, success doesn't come that easily.

For most of us, scouting and success in the outdoors go hand in hand. Knowing the land, understanding animal behavior, and putting in the hours makes all the difference. It doesn't guarantee success, but it sure tips the odds in your favor. That being said, scouting isn't just about putting in the work; it's about learning from it. How often do we walk the land, mark the rubs and scrapes, and study wind patterns, only to realize mid-season that our assumptions were way off? While tech advancements and experience have helped me scout more efficiently, one truth remains clear. Preparation matters, but growth usually comes through persistence, not instant results. Sometimes, we find ourselves sitting in the wrong spot, learning through trial and error—just like in life.

Proverbs 3:5 tells us to "Trust in the Lord with all your heart and lean not on your own understanding." Just like scouting teaches us to observe, adapt, and trust our instincts, life calls us to rely on God's guidance. We may pour time into planning, studying, and preparing, but there will always be unknowns. God sees the bigger picture when we can only see a fragment of the map. When we're uncertain or overwhelmed, He invites us to trust that He's already paved the way ahead of us.

That kind of trust isn't always easy. Maybe you've faced a season where nothing seemed to align, and your best efforts felt fruitless. Those moments can feel frustrating and even discouraging. Yet, God uses these times to refine us, strengthen our faith, and prepare us for the opportunities He's aligning. As Romans 8:28 says, "And we know that in all things God works for the good of those who love him, who have been called according to his purpose."

Even when the terrain seems unfamiliar or the path unclear, God is working for our good.

No amount of e-scouting, trail cameras, or preparation can fully eliminate the need for adjustments. Conditions change, and flexibility is crucial. Similarly, God doesn't reveal every detail of His plan up front. He calls us to step out in faith, trusting His guidance even when we can't see what's ahead.

Throughout life, I've often tried to be in the driver's seat, but each time, I've come to the same conclusion that true success comes when we let go of control. The peace we seek is found in trusting the One who knows every detail. When we commit ourselves to the Lord, trust in His wisdom, and allow Him to guide us, we end up exactly where we need to be, experiencing the peace that surpasses all understanding.

1 M.O.A.

Letting go of control isn't weakness—it's wisdom. You can scout, plan, and prepare all you want, but if you're not willing to trust God with the outcome, you're still holding the wheel. Faith means stepping forward even when the next turn isn't clear. It's not about having all the answers. It's about knowing the One who does. Don't just trust God when the path is smooth. Trust Him when the trail disappears.

Mission: Develop a habit of seeking God's guidance before making decisions. Just as scouting a hunting area increases your chances of success, regularly seeking God's wisdom equips you to navigate life's challenges with clarity and confidence.

Obedience: Actively surrender your plans to God by making prayer your priority, not your last resort. Spend time in prayer before making important decisions, meditate on Scripture for wisdom, and be open to godly counsel from those around you.

Accuracy: Progress becomes evident when faith directs your decisions rather than impulse. Instead of moving without direction, you'll walk with confidence, knowing your steps are aligned with God's will, bringing clarity and purpose.

PRAYER

Heavenly Father, thank You for being my constant guide and protector. I surrender my plans to You, trusting in Your perfect wisdom and timing. Help me rely fully on You, even when the path ahead feels unclear. Give me the courage to follow wherever You lead, and the discernment to recognize Your direction in my life. Strengthen my faith so that I may walk confidently in the steps You have prepared for me. In Jesus' name, Amen.

DAY 3
SIGHTING IN

VERSE

The prudent see danger and take refuge, but the simple keep going and pay the penalty.
Proverbs 27:12

THE TARGET

Success in the field isn't just about having the right gear or perfecting your technique. It's about guarding against unseen dangers—those moments when complacency or carelessness can lead to painful consequences. Proverbs 27:12 reminds us that wisdom is found in recognizing potential dangers and taking steps to avoid them. Whether in the field or in life, a moment of neglect can cost you. Today, we'll consider how to stay alert, prepared, and intentional about guarding our hearts, minds, and decisions.

ZEROED IN

Before every season, sighting in your firearm or bow is essential. You can't just assume last year's setup is still dialed in—every load, every adjustment, every change needs to be accounted for. This time, I was sighting in my shotgun for turkey season. I had a new load to test, and everything looked promising. I was set up in front of a homemade "trap" designed to catch the shot. The setup was about five feet high, built with railroad ties stacked on all sides. To make it extra secure, dirt was mounded on top of everything, and inside the trap, a steel plate was angled downward to deflect pellets or bullets into the ground. It was a solid system. I had used it plenty of times without any issues.

I lined up the shot, confident that everything was in place. I squeezed the trigger, and everything seemed normal—until it wasn't. Before I could even register what had happened, a sharp sting hit me in the face, just below my eye. One of the pellets had ricocheted right back at me. For a split second, it was like time slowed down. I reached up instinctively, half-expecting to feel something worse. The pellet had missed my eye by maybe half an inch. No blood, just a dull pain and the realization of how differently things could have gone. The most sobering part? I wasn't wearing any protective eye gear. I had convinced myself I didn't need it. After all, I'd done this plenty of times before. The trap was built tough, the angle was right, and everything had worked fine every other time I'd used it. But none of that mattered when one pellet caught the wrong angle.

As I stood there with my hand still on my face, I couldn't stop thinking about how close I'd come to disaster. It didn't matter how many times I'd done it before—one unexpected moment was all it took to remind me that preparation and precaution aren't optional. They're essential. It was a reminder that even when everything looks safe and routine, the unexpected can still happen. No matter how ready we think we are, there are moments when things don't go as planned—and those moments can change everything in an instant.

We're all guilty of it—getting comfortable when nothing's gone wrong for a while. Spiritually, we do the same thing. We read the Bible less because life feels fine. We let prayer slide because there's no crisis. We drop our guard because nothing's attacked us—yet. But Proverbs 27:12 warns us, "The prudent see danger and take refuge, but the simple keep going and pay the penalty."

That's where we mess up. We assume that because things have been quiet, they'll stay that way. But spiritual danger doesn't announce itself. It doesn't come with flashing lights or loud warnings. It's often subtle, creeping in where we least expect it. And when we're not spiritually grounded, when we let our guard down because we feel comfortable, that's often when we're most vulnerable.

Think about Adam and Eve in the Garden of Eden. They had everything—peace, provision, and a direct relationship with God. But in a moment of vulnerability, they listened to a voice that questioned what God had said. The enemy didn't rush in with force; he worked through subtle temptation and distortion. It wasn't one dramatic fall, but a slow unraveling that began with letting their guard down. By the time they realized what had happened, the damage was done. Their story is one of the earliest and clearest warnings in Scripture—reminding us how quickly things can fall apart when we stop standing on truth.

Spiritual alertness isn't about scrambling to respond after things go wrong. It's about building daily habits that guard your heart before the battle even begins. Prayer, Scripture, and accountability aren't just for crisis moments—they're your everyday gear, whether you feel the need or not. The moment you stop staying spiritually sharp is the moment you become vulnerable. Like Adam and Eve in the garden, we often don't realize we've let our guard down until the damage is already done.

We assume that because things feel stable, they'll stay that way. But complacency is a dangerous trap. It dulls our senses and blinds us to the threats that are quietly closing in. So where are you leaving yourself unprotected? Is it in your thought life? The relationships you're allowing to drift? The habits you've stopped guarding? Are you assuming that because things feel fine now, they'll stay that way?

Don't wait for an unguarded moment that could change everything. Take refuge now—stay protected and sighted in to God before the shot ever goes off.

1 M.O.A.

It's not always the big dangers that take us down. Sometimes, it's the small things we overlook—the moments when we assume everything is fine because nothing's gone wrong yet. But those are the moments where we're most vulnerable. When we stop checking our surroundings, stop reinforcing our defenses, and stop paying attention to what could go wrong, we leave ourselves wide open to unexpected hits.

Mission: Pay attention to the little things. Don't just focus on what's obvious—look at the habits, attitudes, and areas in your life where you've gotten comfortable. Where have you stopped being intentional? Where have you assumed safety when you should have stayed on guard?

Obedience: If you've been coasting in prayer, commit to a consistent time. If you've ignored conviction about something, deal with it now. Don't wait for a spiritual ricochet to wake you up—take action before it's too late.

Accuracy: You'll know you're growing when you're not just reacting to danger, but actively staying alert to it. A heart grounded in God's truth doesn't flinch when the unexpected happens—it stands steady because it's been trained to trust.

PRAYER

Dear Jesus, I know it's easy to let my guard down when life feels safe. I get comfortable when nothing's going wrong, and I forget how quickly things can change. I don't want to assume I'm prepared when I've been coasting spiritually. Help me to stay alert. Open my eyes to the areas where I've grown careless, including my habits, my thoughts, and my relationships. Show me where I've left myself vulnerable, and give me the discipline to strengthen those weak spots. Teach me to take refuge in You before the danger comes, not after it hits. Keep my heart sharp, my mind clear, and my faith grounded so that when the unexpected happens, I'm standing firm in You. In Jesus' name, Amen.

DAY 4
PLANTING WITH PURPOSE

VERSE

Remember this: Whoever sows sparingly will also reap sparingly, and whoever sows generously will also reap generously.
2 Corinthians 9:6

THE TARGET

2 Corinthians 9:6 says that the more generously and intentionally we sow, the greater the harvest we can expect—not just in the field, but in every area of life. The seeds we plant today will shape the harvest of tomorrow, impacting not only our own lives but those around us. Consider how the seeds we sow—whether in our relationships, our work, or our walk with Christ—can bear fruit when planted generously and faithfully.

ZEROED IN

Throughout my life, I've been blessed with opportunities to hunt on family farms and private land, as well as spending plenty of time on public land. Each experience has its own charm, but hunting on private property offers something uniquely attractive. It gives you the freedom to manage the land and design food plots to attract and sustain wildlife. For most of my hunting years, though, I never gave much thought to planting food plots. Living in the Midwest, surrounded by corn and soybean fields, it didn't seem necessary—deer already had plenty to eat, and we saw them regularly. But a couple of years ago, my buddy and I decided to give it a shot. With access to over 550 acres, we thought food plots might help concentrate deer movement in specific areas and improve our chances of choosing the right spot to sit.

That summer, we identified three promising areas in the timber to create food plots. We spent days clearing trees, leveling the ground, and preparing the soil. It was exhausting work, but the vision of hunting over lush, green food plots kept us motivated. When it came time to plant, we grabbed bags of seed and got to work, confident that all our preparation would pay off by hunting season. This is where our inexperience became clear. We had no idea how food plot seed mixtures were proportioned. Many bags are loaded with "filler" plants—grasses and low-quality seeds that grow quickly but offer little nutritional value or attraction for deer. The good stuff—like clover, brassicas, or chicory—typically makes up only a small percentage of the mix. In hindsight, we probably should've spent as much time reading the seed bag as we did clearing trees. But let's be honest, the lush field on the packaging was way more alluring than the tiny print on the back of the bag.

When the plants started to grow, we realized our mistake. The plots looked green and full at first, but as the season progressed, the filler plants dominated. The few good plants we'd sown struggled to survive among the aggressive fillers. All the time, energy, and effort we had poured into these plots felt somewhat wasted. It was frustrating, but it was also a lesson learned. Preparation matters, and so does the quality of what you plant. Just like in hunting or farming, the same is true in life—if we don't take the time to sow the right seeds, we can't expect a meaningful harvest.

In life, we're constantly planting seeds, through our relationships, our work, our habits, and our walk with Christ. But here's the challenge. Sowing generously isn't enough if what we're sowing lacks depth or direction. Like those filler plants, we can pour effort into things that look good on the surface but offer little spiritual value. 2 Corinthians 9:6 reminds us, "Whoever sows sparingly will also reap sparingly, and whoever sows generously will also reap generously." But generosity must be paired with discernment. What are you actually sowing? Are your investments of time, energy, and focus filled with spiritual purpose, or are they crowded with distractions, obligations, or things that simply don't bear lasting fruit?

Galatians 6:7-9 teaches us, "A man reaps what he sows… Let us not become weary in doing good, for at the proper time we will reap a harvest if we do not give up." This passage reminds us that God's timing is perfect and encourages us to persevere in planting seeds of faith, love, and generosity—even when the results aren't immediate. Sometimes, sowing generously can feel costly, but God promises that the harvest will come if we remain faithful.

Much like our food plots that year, the filler plants in life can crowd out what truly matters. Busyness, misplaced priorities, and distractions can take over, leaving little room for spiritual growth or meaningful connections. The good news is that God is the ultimate food plot designer. When we trust Him with the process and are intentional about planting the right seeds, He brings the growth. Are you sowing seeds of faith, generosity, and love, or are filler plants like busyness, distractions, and overloaded work schedules taking over?

1 M.O.A.

Just like a food plot needs the right seed to bear fruit, your spiritual life needs intentional planting. Be generous, yes—but also discerning. Make sure what you're sowing aligns with God's Word and purpose, not just your own expectations.

Mission: Approach every action, decision, and investment of time with intentionality. Consider what you are planting in your life—your habits, relationships, and spiritual disciplines. Sow seeds that will produce lasting, God-honoring fruit.

Obedience: Choose one relationship in your life where you can intentionally plant a seed of encouragement, grace, or reconciliation, while also cultivating a new habit that strengthens your spiritual walk. This could mean reaching out to someone in need, offering forgiveness, or making a habit of prayer or Scripture before you engage with others.

Accuracy: Evidence of your faithfulness will show in the fruit of your actions. When you plant with purpose, you'll begin to see the results of your consistency—whether it's stronger relationships, spiritual maturity, or unexpected blessings that come from remaining faithful in the small things.

PRAYER

Lord, thank You for the reminder that the seeds I plant today can grow into something meaningful and lasting. Help me to sow generously and with purpose, trusting that You will bring growth in Your perfect timing. Teach me to invest my heart and actions in ways that reflect Your love and truth. Guide me to focus on what matters most, strengthening my faith as I rely on Your guidance and know that You are always faithful. In Jesus' name, Amen.

DAY 5
THE PERFECT SETUP

VERSE

Therefore everyone who hears these words of mine and puts them into practice is like a wise man who built his house on the rock. The rain came down, the streams rose, and the winds blew and beat against that house; yet it did not fall, because it had its foundation on the rock.
Matthew 7:24-25

THE TARGET

Jesus teaches us the importance of building a solid foundation for our lives. The wise man didn't just hear the words of Jesus; he lived them out, allowing His teachings to shape his actions. When the storms of life come, as they inevitably do, it is this foundation that keeps us standing firm. This verse challenges us to not just listen to God's Word, but to actively apply it, ensuring that our lives are built on the unshakable rock of His truth. Take a moment today to consider where your foundation lies—are you firmly rooted in Christ, or depending on something less stable?

ZEROED IN

One of my favorite parts of the offseason is putting up or moving stands. There's something deeply satisfying about scouting, strategizing your setup, and picking that perfect tree where it all comes together. Every hunter has their own philosophy about stand placement, and believe me, I've heard them all. Some of my buddies are die-hard about their methods. Should it be a ladder stand, a climber, or a saddle? Do you go with an elevated blind? Should you paint it to blend in, or leave it alone because deer will just get used to it? Then there are debates about how high to place the stand, whether to sit tight to a trail or back off into the timber, and even what type of tree is ideal. Let's just say I've been part of some spirited debates.

Personally, I'd like to think I fall somewhere in the middle. I have my preferences, sure, but I try to stay flexible. I typically lean toward ladder stands—they feel secure and can be easier to use (especially when you're packing more snacks than gear). But I also use climbers and elevated blinds when the situation calls for it. In most cases, I prefer to stay fairly concealed, making sure I've got three or four solid shooting lanes. If I'm hunting a field edge or food plot, I like to set my stand back 5–15 yards into the timber, keeping myself tucked away while still in range. In the woods, I'll hang a stand about 10–30 yards off a main trail to give myself a little buffer. Many of my preferences come from watching my family and our old family friends as I grew up—men who spent a lifetime figuring out what worked and what didn't in the woods. Over time, I've adapted their methods to fit my own style and experiences.

Some properties make stand placement pretty straightforward. One of my favorite places to hunt in Oregon, has a wild apple tree right in the middle of a secluded opening in the timber. During archery season, it is an absolute magnet for deer. Within the timber is also three or four well-worn "highways" where deer traffic is guaranteed. Sitting in any of those spots almost feels like cheating—we'd see 30+ deer every time we hunted. Some of my favorite properties here in the Midwest have ranged from 300 to 600 acres, and they require a lot more thought and effort. I usually put up multiple stands in an area to account for changing winds and different funnels or food sources.

Even with all that planning, surprises still happen. One time, I dozed off in a ladder stand (it happens more often than I'd like to admit), and I woke to the faint sound of rustling leaves beneath me. Slowly, I opened my eyes, and there he was—a solid 8-point buck standing directly under my stand. I was a teenager at the time, and he looked like a true trophy. My bow was hanging next to me, but he was too close for me to make a move without spooking him. I decided to enjoy the moment, soaking in the experience, and hoping I'd see him again another day.

Despite all the strategizing and perfect stand placements, hunting has a way of keeping you humble. Sometimes the wind shifts, the action moves 100 yards away, or the deer show up somewhere completely unexpected. It's a reminder that even the best-laid plans don't guarantee the outcome. The same is true in life. Even when you've prepared faithfully and done everything right, surprises still come. That's why your foundation matters so much. When your life is rooted in Christ, you're not just ready to stand firm—you're also equipped to adapt with wisdom, patience, and trust in God's plan.

Matthew 7:24-25 reminds us of the importance of building on a solid foundation. Jesus says that those who hear His words and put them into practice are like a wise man who built his house on the rock. When the storms came, the house stood firm because it was built on the right foundation. In hunting, you don't just pick a random tree and hope for the best. You study the terrain, consider the wind, and make adjustments based on the environment. Similarly, in life, we're called to align our choices with God's Word, ensuring that we're rooted in His truth. When we do, we're able to withstand whatever storms come our way.

Proverbs 24:27 gives us further wisdom, saying, "Put your outdoor work in order and get your fields ready; after that, build your house." This verse speaks to the importance of careful planning and intentional action. Rushing through decisions or ignoring the details can leave us unprepared and vulnerable when difficulties arise. But when we take the time to plan, seek God's guidance, and build our foundation on Him, we're prepared not just for success but for resilience, no matter what comes our way.

The beautiful part is that even when we realize we've set our "stand" in the wrong spot, God's grace is still there to meet us. Maybe you've been "sitting in the wrong tree" lately—pursuing goals or priorities that aren't aligned with His plan for your life. The good news is that it's never too late to reposition yourself. Remember, the right spot isn't always the easiest or most obvious—it's the one that positions you to grow in faith and experience the fullness of God's purpose for your life.

> **1 M.O.A.**
>
> Placing your stand in the right spot is about more than just location—it's about awareness, adaptability, and the right approach. In the same way, building your life on a strong foundation requires intentional effort, thoughtful reflection, and trusting God to guide your steps. When you root yourself in Christ, you're not only prepared for life's challenges but positioned to thrive and grow.
>
> **Mission:** Position yourself for spiritual growth and success by aligning your life with God's guidance. Just as a well-planned setup increases your chances in the field, intentionally seeking God's direction places you in the best position to experience His purpose for your life.
>
> **Obedience:** Take steps to remove distractions and realign your focus on God. This could mean restructuring your daily routine to prioritize time in His Word, surrounding yourself with godly influences, or letting go of habits that are keeping you from growing spiritually.
>
> **Accuracy:** As you seek God's guidance and align your actions with His truth, you'll find yourself making decisions that honor Him, even when circumstances are unpredictable. Just as hunters adjust their approach based on changing conditions, spiritual accuracy means being willing to pivot and trust God's direction, knowing that He's leading you exactly where you need to be.

PRAYER

Dear Jesus, thank You for being my firm foundation, guiding my steps and anchoring me in Your truth. Help me to build my life on You, trusting Your Word and following Your lead in every decision I make. Show me where I need to realign my focus and strengthen my foundation, and give me the wisdom and courage to take those steps. When life brings challenges and uncertainties, remind me that I can stand strong because You are with me. In Jesus' name, Amen.

DAY 6
TRUST BUILT ON BOUNDARIES

VERSE

Love the Lord your God with all your heart and with all your soul and with all your mind and with all your strength.' The second is this: 'Love your neighbor as yourself.' There is no commandment greater than these.
Mark 12:30-31

THE TARGET

Jesus lays out the two greatest commandments, calling us to love God with everything we have and to love others with the same depth of care. This commandment isn't just about feeling love; it's about living it out in action. Loving God fully involves every aspect of our being—our heart, soul, mind, and strength—while loving our neighbors calls us to extend that same sacrificial love to those around us. Today, reflect on how you can embody both commands in your life, with a focus on loving your neighbor. Are there areas where your love for others could be deepened or made more intentional?

ZEROED IN

I've been blessed with some incredible neighbors over the years—the kind who lend equipment, help lift box blinds, or show up with a tractor when a fallen tree blocks your trail. One guy near a property we had access to used to bring over his skid steer without us even asking. That kind of neighborly spirit makes hunting more than a hobby—it becomes community. It reminds you that the outdoors isn't just about the harvest, but the people you share it with. However, not all neighborly expereinces are that easy.

A few seasons back, we gained access to a beautiful 350-acre property—mature timber, great funnels, consistent trail cam activity. On paper, it had everything. But almost immediately, we started running into problems. During our initial scouting trip, we found multiple bait stations—corn and mineral piles—strategically placed about 20–40 yards from permanent stands. That raised a red flag, especially since baiting is illegal in Indiana. The landowner didn't hunt and hadn't leased the land to anyone else. We were left with a troubling question. Who was doing this?

We contacted the DNR, reported everything, and followed their advice to steer clear of the baited zones. But nothing changed. Over the next few weeks, the bait piles were refilled, and no enforcement followed. We tried to focus on hunting legally and ethically, and despite the situation, we had a decent season.

The next year, though, things escalated. The baiting stopped—but now gear started disappearing. Tree stands vanished. Trail cams were stolen or smashed. One morning, we even found 2 deer carcasses dumped into a sinkhole. It was upsetting, not just because of what was lost, but because of how powerless it felt. We reported those things too, but again, nothing came of it. And while we had strong suspicions about one individual, we never had proof. Just patterns. Glimpses. A truck parked too close to the fence. A figure cutting across the property early in the morning.

What started as a frustrating hunting season turned into something more personal. My thoughts started spiraling. I replayed every incident. Every missing treestand. Every stolen blind. I convinced myself I knew who was responsible—and in my heart, I let that suspicion grow into bitterness.

And that's when I had to confront something much deeper than property lines or stolen gear. Jesus said, "love your neighbor as yourself." It's one of the two greatest commandments. What happens, then, when your neighbor isn't clearly defined? What happens when you're not even sure who hurt you, but you're angry anyway? What if your "neighbor" is a stranger or worse, someone you've made into a villain in your own mind?

That experience forced me to wrestle with the weight of Christ's words. Loving your neighbor isn't just about helping the guy next door shovel his driveway or loan a tool. It's about checking your own heart when things go sideways—praying for the person you suspect but can't accuse, choosing restraint when you want to confront. It's about remembering that justice belongs to God, not you.

The reality is, I will never know who was behind those actions. But I know exactly what was growing in my own heart, and I know God was calling me to something higher. Love isn't passive, and it's not naive. But it is patient. It's respectful. It's humble. Loving your neighbor means refusing to let bitterness set the tone. It means choosing peace in a situation where you don't get closure. It means reflecting Christ—not only when you're certain, but especially when you're not.

And that's the deeper truth behind Jesus' command. "Neighbor" doesn't just mean the person who lives next door. It means anyone God places in your path. Anyone who tests your patience, challenges your assumptions, or crosses your boundaries. Anyone you're tempted to judge without all the facts. Because loving them isn't about their behavior—it's about your obedience.

1 M.O.A.

Jesus didn't call us to love our neighbors only when it's convenient or comfortable; He called us to love them even when they challenge us. That means responding with kindness and respect, praying for them when frustration takes over, and trusting God with justice. Loving your neighbor doesn't always feel natural, but through His Spirit, we can reflect Christ's character in every interaction.

Mission: We are called to honor God by loving others as He loves us, especially when it's challenging. This means being a source of grace, patience, and integrity, showing His love to all people, regardless of how they treat us.

Obedience: Make a conscious effort to extend kindness to a difficult neighbor, coworker, or acquaintance. Whether it's a simple act of respect, a genuine conversation, or praying for them, choose to reflect Christ's love in a tangible way.

Accuracy: You'll know you're walking in obedience when your response to others—especially difficult people—reflects God's love rather than frustration. The true measure of spiritual growth isn't how we treat those who are easy to love, but how we handle those who test our patience and character.

PRAYER

Heavenly Father, thank You for reminding me of the importance of loving those around me, even when it feels challenging. Help me to reflect Your character in my actions and responses, and remind me that they are in my life for a reason. Soften my heart toward those who test my patience, and teach me to show kindness and grace, just as You've shown me. Give me the strength to love not through my own limited ability, but through the abundant love and grace You've poured into my life. May my words and actions glorify You and plant seeds of Your truth in the lives of those around me. In Jesus' name, Amen.

DAY 7
FIRESIDE FELLOWSHIP

VERSE

And let us consider how we may spur one another on toward love and good deeds, not giving up meeting together, as some are in the habit of doing, but encouraging one another—and all the more as you see the Day approaching.
Hebrews 10:24-25

THE TARGET

In Hebrews 10:24-25, we are reminded of the power and importance of community. We're not meant to walk this journey of faith alone. Instead, we're called to encourage and support each other, spurring one another on toward love and good deeds. In a world where it's easy to become isolated or discouraged, staying connected with others in faith is essential. As we come together, we find strength, accountability, and the encouragement we need to keep pressing forward. Think about the people God has placed in your life—are you investing in those relationships, encouraging them, and allowing yourself to be encouraged?

ZEROED IN

Hunting and fishing have been a part of my life for as long as I can remember. Up until my early 20s, it was always a shared tradition. Whether it was just my immediate family or family friends tagging along, I never hunted or fished alone. It's always been about shared experiences, learning from those who had done it before me, and spending time together outdoors. But in the last several years, things changed. As life got busier and family dynamics shifted, I found myself hunting and fishing alone more often than not. At first, I didn't mind. I've always enjoyed solitude—the quiet, the stillness, and the escape from distractions. But over time, something started to feel off. I realized just how much I missed the camaraderie, the shared excitement of the hunt, and the late-night conversations around a fire. I was still just as passionate—scouting, setting up stands, strategizing—but there was a noticeable gap. No one to bounce ideas off. No one to swap trail cam pics with. No one to give a hard time when they completely botch a shot—and no one to return the favor if I, hypothetically, ever did the same (which, for the record, I haven't). It wasn't enough to make me stop hunting, but it made me realize how much I had taken those moments of fellowship for granted.

Eventually, those solo seasons began to feel more isolating than peaceful. But then, everything changed. I got connected with a group of six guys, and I don't say this lightly—it completely transformed the way I view hunting. For the first time in years, I wasn't doing it alone. These guys were just as dedicated—just as obsessed with the details and excited about the little things that make hunting special. And for the first time ever, I experienced something I had never really had before, a real deer camp. Now, if you've never been to one, let me set the scene. With over 550 acres at our disposal, our camp was everything I dreamed of as a kid. Three travel trailers, a four-by-five-foot fire pit, a grill, a cabana with string lights, a TV hooked up for late-night football games, all our trucks lined up, and ATVs scattered around camp. The nights were just as important as the mornings—we'd sit around the fire, swap stories, talk about past seasons, and strategize for the morning hunt. It was a mix of wisdom, laughter, and friendly jabs.

Here's what really stuck with me. For the first time in a long time, I felt connected not just to the experience but to the people around me. That's when it hit me. We were never meant to do life alone. There's something in us, especially as men, that makes us think we can handle everything on our own. We convince ourselves that we don't need help, that isolation is strength, that being self-sufficient is the goal. And while independence has its place, we were never designed to live apart from community.

Hebrews 10:24-25 encourages us to actively support and motivate one another to live out love and good deeds. It emphasizes the importance of remaining connected and regularly gathering with others in faith, especially as we approach the return of Christ, so that we can continue encouraging each other. Fellowship isn't optional. It's essential. The devil wants us isolated, alone, easy to manipulate, easier to break down. When we separate ourselves from others, we lose the encouragement, the accountability, and the sharpening that only comes from being around like-minded people. Proverbs 27:17 puts it plainly with the words, "As iron sharpens iron, so one person sharpens another."

I've seen too many people drift, not because they lost faith, but because they lost connection with those who kept them grounded. That slow fade starts with "I'll catch up with them later" and turns into months, then years of distance. Before they know it, they're struggling alone, convinced that no one would understand. Maybe you're in that place right now. Maybe you've been hunting—or living life—alone for a while. Maybe it's been easier to keep to yourself, to avoid the effort of connection. But here's the truth. You weren't meant to go at it alone. God created you for fellowship—to be strengthened by others and to strengthen them in return. Don't let pride or busyness keep you from the relationships that will strengthen you. Whether it's hunting buddies, a Bible study group, or just a couple of solid friends, make the effort to connect. Build relationships that sharpen you, push you, and remind you that you're not in this alone. Because at the end of the day, life—like a good hunt—is meant to be shared.

1 M.O.A.

God created us for connection—not just for the good times, but for the challenges as well. Think about your best hunting or fishing experiences—chances are you weren't alone. When we isolate ourselves, we miss out on the encouragement, accountability, and wisdom that God designed us to have through community. Take a moment today to reflect: Are you investing in the people God has placed in your life? Are you allowing them to sharpen and encourage you, or have you been walking alone?

Mission: Make intentional space for meaningful fellowship with God and others. Just as stories, laughter, and deep conversations are shared around a campfire, our faith grows when we take time to connect with God and with those He has placed in our lives.

Obedience: Set aside time this week to slow down and be present. Whether it's having an intentional conversation with a friend, gathering with fellow believers, or seeking solitude for reflection, prioritize meaningful connection over distraction.

Accuracy: Spiritual maturity becomes evident as your relationships deepen, your time with God becomes more consistent, and you begin to see fellowship not as an obligation, but as a necessary and fulfilling part of your faith journey. True connection leaves you encouraged, refreshed, and strengthened to continue walking in God's purpose.

PRAYER

Lord, thank You for the gift of community. You designed us to walk this life together, encouraging and strengthening one another. Help me to seek out and invest in the relationships You have placed in my life. Show me where I need to reconnect, where I need to invest more intentionally, and where I need to be open to new friendships You are placing in my life. Keep me from the temptation of isolation, and surround me with people who sharpen my faith and point me toward You. Thank You for the bonds of fellowship that remind me I'm never alone. In Jesus' name, Amen.

DAY 8
THE MORNING JITTERS

VERSE

Do not be anxious about anything, but in every situation, by prayer and petition, with thanksgiving, present your requests to God. And the peace of God, which transcends all understanding, will guard your hearts and your minds in Christ Jesus.
Philippians 4:6-7

THE TARGET

It's easy to let anxiousness take over, but Philippians 4:6–7 reminds us to bring every worry to God through prayer. Instead of stressing over what we can't control, we're called to trust Him—knowing that His peace will guard our hearts and minds. Today, focus on surrendering those nerves, embracing the moment, and resting in the confidence that, no matter what happens, you're exactly where you need to be.

ZEROED IN

Ever since I was a kid, the morning of a hunt has always brought a rush of excitement and nerves. Even now, just thinking about it makes my legs feel a little shaky. The anticipation, the excitement, and yes, a little bit of nervousness—it all hits at once. It's like my nerves have been gearing up for opening day just as much as I have. Over the years, I've gotten better at managing it, but let's just say it still takes some effort.

I often think back to one particular morning when I was ten years old. It was opening day of gun season, and we were pulling up to our hunting property well before daylight. The entrance sat right off a four-lane highway, but once you got past the first gate, the land stretched back far enough that the sounds of passing cars faded away. That morning, my excitement was at an all-time high—but so was my anxiousness. It was my first year carrying my own shotgun, and I was both thrilled and a little nervous. Would the deer show up? Would I make the right call when the moment came? All those thoughts raced through my head as we rolled through the gate and into the pasture.

While my family and friends unloaded the ATVs, I tried to focus on getting my gear together. But then, my nerves hit me hard—so hard that I suddenly had a very urgent need to find a bathroom. And by "bathroom," I mean the great outdoors. Panicked, I ran up to them and said it was an emergency. Without hesitation, they reached into the side of the truck door, grabbed a wad of napkins, and handed them to me. Then, as calmly as ever, they pointed to a fence post and said, "Run over there, lean against it, and take care of business."

I didn't have time to question their advice. This was a full-scale emergency. I sprinted to the wooden post, got into position, and just as I was in the middle of my unfortunate predicament, a flood of cars came barreling down the highway. That's when it hit me. The fence post? Yeah, it wasn't in some nice, secluded spot. It was right on the edge of the road. There I was, a ten-year-old kid, in the dark, fully illuminated by the high beams of passing vehicles, giving early morning commuters an experience they probably never forgot.

That moment became a core memory, one I can laugh about now. But let's just say it wasn't the last time my nerves got the best of me. Over the years, I've earned a reputation for being a little too familiar with nature's restroom, and I never step into the woods without the proper supplies. In fact, it's happened enough that my hunting buddies don't even ask questions anymore. One particularly humbling experience happened a couple of years ago while elk hunting in the Pacific Northwest.

Let's just say I found myself in a less-than-ideal situation when, mid-emergency, I heard a deer higher up the ravine blowing at me. If there's ever been a moment to feel completely exposed in the great outdoors, that was it. After all these years, my anxiousness still sneaks up on me. Not as often as it did when I was a kid, but it happens.

Anxiousness has a way of creeping in when we least expect it. Sometimes it's over small things, like opening day jitters, but other times it's about much bigger things—decisions, responsibilities, or situations we can't control. The morning of a hunt isn't all that different from the way we approach life. We can prepare, plan, and study everything ahead of time, but there will always be unknowns. That's why Philippians 4:6-7 speaks directly to those moments of nervous anticipation. Instead of allowing anxiousness to take over, this passage encourages us to bring our worries to God. When we do, He replaces our fear with His peace—a peace that doesn't always make sense but is powerful enough to steady our hearts.

Looking back, I realize that if I had trusted God more that morning, maybe I wouldn't have been so overwhelmed. Maybe I wouldn't have let my nerves take over. Maybe I would've been able to laugh in the moment instead of only afterward. Life's like that, too. We'll always face situations that make us uneasy. When anxiety shows up, we still have a choice—let it rule our hearts, or hand it over to God and trust that He's already gone ahead of us.

So the next time you're in the truck on the way to your stand, nerves kicking in, what-if questions swirling in your head—pause. Take a deep breath. Pray. Thank God for the opportunity, for the moment you're in, and ask Him to replace your anxiousness with His peace. The deer might show up, or they might not. Either way, you can rest in the confidence that God is in control.

1 M.O.A.

Anxiousness can sneak up on us in different ways—whether it's the anticipation of a hunt, the weight of responsibilities, or the uncertainty of what's ahead. Yet worry was never meant to be our default. God invites us to trade our anxiety for His peace, a peace that doesn't come from knowing every outcome but from trusting the One who does. Just like scouting, planning, and preparation can ease nerves before a hunt, spending time in prayer and leaning into God's promises prepares our hearts to face whatever comes with confidence.

Mission: Develop a habit of turning to God when anxiety creeps in. Just as opening-day nerves are natural but manageable, so are the worries we face in everyday life. The key is not to let fear control us, but to trust God in every moment.

Obedience: When anxious thoughts arise, replace them with prayer and truth. Memorize a Bible verse that reminds you of God's peace (like Philippians 4:6-7) and repeat it whenever worry tries to take hold. Take a few deep breaths, refocus your thoughts on Him, and step forward in confidence.

Accuracy: You'll recognize spiritual growth when your first instinct in moments of stress is to seek God's presence instead of dwelling on fear. When you find yourself choosing faith over worry, leaning into prayer over panic, and stepping forward with confidence in His plan, you'll know you're moving in the right direction.

PRAYER

Heavenly Father, Thank You for reminding me that I don't have to carry my worries alone. Too often, I let anxious thoughts take over when I should be placing my trust in You. Help me to surrender my fears, big and small, and to find peace in knowing that You are in control. Replace my worries with confidence in Your plan, and steady my heart with the peace that only You can give. No matter what happens today or in the future, I trust that You are leading me. In Jesus' name, Amen.

DAY 9
THE POWER OF STILLNESS

VERSE

Be still, and know that I am God; I will be exalted among the nations, I will be exalted in the earth.
Psalm 46:10

THE TARGET

Just like in the woods, where movement and noise can work against you, in life, distractions can keep you from hearing God's voice. The world is loud—full of pressures, responsibilities, and constant demands for your attention. But God calls us to stillness, not because He needs silence, but because we do. In the quiet, we find clarity. In the stillness, we learn trust. Today, take time to slow down. Be present. Be still. And in that stillness, recognize that God is in control.

ZEROED IN

If you've ever hunted with others, you know that stillness doesn't come naturally to everyone. There's always that one guy who just can't sit still—the one who fidgets, forgets how to whisper, stretches at the worst time, and somehow always has the loudest snack wrappers known to man. Don't get me wrong. When I'm hunting with someone, I enjoy a quiet conversation every now and then, depending on the situation. But I've always been able to settle in, slow down, and stay still for as long as it takes. Patience and stillness have always come naturally to me. My family friend Ben, on the other hand, hunts a little differently.

Ben is the kind of person you can't help but admire. A devoted husband, father, and man of faith, he leads with kindness and integrity in everything he does. When I was 13, he gave me a summer job working for his painting business, and for the next nine years, I spent my summers painting houses alongside him. No matter where he was—on the job, at home, or in the woods—he carried himself with the same steady kindness and respect.

That being said, you always knew when Ben arrived at a job site. Not because of the cherry bomb exhaust on his baby blue Chevy Corvair, but because he was always whistling or humming his favorite tune. Hunting with him was no different. Once he got his gear on, he'd take off into the woods, still humming and whistling like he had just pulled up to a house we were about to paint. I remember sitting in our box blind together during gun season, watching the woods wake up around us. Just as everything settled into that peaceful morning stillness, I'd hear it—click, click—the sound of Ben unlocking the lid on his thermos, followed by a long, satisfied ahhh as he took a sip of coffee. It never failed to make me smile.

Ben wasn't there to stress over the hunt—he was there to enjoy it. He whistled on the way in, hummed when we sat down, and every so often, he'd suggest a midday "walkabout" just to stretch his legs and see what was moving. If we weren't together, by 11 a.m., I'd usually see him wandering through the woods or across the field, simply happy to be outside. He grew up bird hunting in South Dakota, so maybe some of those habits carried over. While our approaches were different, one thing was certain—Ben always found a way to fill his tags.

Looking back, I don't regret a single moment hunting with him. Because while Ben may not have been the quietest hunting buddy, he taught me something far more important in life than sitting still in a blind—he taught me the value of slowing down to hear God's voice. Ben may have filled the woods with sound, but in life, he knew how to make space for what truly mattered.

He led with patience, listened when it counted, and understood when to be still before God. And in the end, that's the kind of stillness that matters most.

True stillness has less to do with physical motion and more to do with the posture of our hearts—learning to pause, listen, and trust. Some of life's most important moments happen in the quiet, where we allow God to speak. Psalm 46:10 says, "Be still, and know that I am God." That verse isn't about physical stillness—it's about inner stillness. It's about resting in God's presence, knowing He is in control. In the same way that movement and noise can ruin a hunt, busyness and distraction can keep us from hearing God's voice. Constant activity can become a camouflage that obscures our vision. Stillness draws the Spirit into clear focus. Hunting teaches us patience, but life demands even more of it. We're constantly rushing, filling every moment with something—tasks, conversations, screens, obligations. The idea of simply being still can feel foreign, maybe even uncomfortable. But when we never slow down, we miss the beauty of what's happening around us. More importantly, we miss what God is trying to say.

> **1 M.O.A.**
>
> Stillness in the woods increases your chances of success, but stillness in life strengthens your faith. When we pause and trust, we create space for God to move, speak, and lead us forward. We live in a world that constantly demands movement and noise, but God calls us to pause, trust, and know that He is in control. When we learn to embrace stillness, we find peace, clarity, and a deeper connection with Him.
>
> **Mission:** Develop the discipline of stillness in your spiritual life. Just as remaining motionless in the field increases your chances of success, learning to quiet your heart before God strengthens your ability to hear His voice and trust in His presence.
>
> **Obedience:** Set aside time each day to be still before God. When doing so, turn off distractions, quiet your thoughts, and focus on prayer or reading His Word. Resist the urge to fill every moment with noise, and instead, practice resting in His presence.

> **Accuracy:** Growth in spiritual stillness becomes evident when moments of quiet no longer feel empty but instead become opportunities to connect with God. True stillness leads to greater clarity, trust, and peace in His presence.

PRAYER

Dear Jesus, thank You for the reminder that stillness is not weakness. It is trust. In a world that constantly pushes me to move, to do, to strive, help me to embrace the power of being still in Your presence. Teach me to quiet my heart, to slow down, and to recognize that You are in control. When I grow restless or anxious, remind me that true peace is found in surrendering to You. Help me not to mistake stillness for inaction, but to see it as an opportunity to grow in faith, to listen for Your voice, and to rest in Your promises. Let my moments of stillness draw me closer to You and shape me into the person You've called me to be. In Jesus' name, Amen.

DAY 10
SCENT CONTROL

VERSE

For we are to God the pleasing aroma of Christ among those who are being saved and those who are perishing.
2 Corinthians 2:15

THE TARGET

As followers of Christ, our lives are meant to reflect Him in such a way that we become a pleasing aroma to God. This isn't about perfection but about living in a way that draws others closer to His love. Whether we're interacting with believers or those who don't yet know Christ, our actions, words, and attitudes should make a difference. As we walk in His grace, let us become a fragrant offering that points others to the saving power of Jesus. Today, focus on how your life is reflecting Christ's love to those around you—are you a sweet aroma that brings glory to God?

ZEROED IN

I probably don't need to tell you about the countless times a doe has circled my stand, caught my scent, and started blowing like crazy—sending an alarm through the woods and alerting every deer in the county. Or the times a coyote got downwind and bolted before we even had a chance to adjust. If you've hunted more than a few times, you know scent can turn a promising hunt into a lost opportunity in seconds. We take every precaution—scent-free soaps, spraying down our gear, playing the wind—but sometimes, no matter how careful we are, the animal's nose wins.

Whenever I think about scent control, one memory always comes to mind, and not for the reason you'd expect.

I was still pretty young, maybe a year or two into hunting on my own, carrying my own gun and sitting in my own stand. It was a brutally cold morning, where every step crunched under your boots. If I had to guess, the temperature was in the teens, especially after the ATV ride to my stand.

The night before, I'd gotten a brand-new bottle of doe pee, packed in a sandwich bag with cotton sticks to hang near my stand. This was my first time using actual deer urine as an attractant. As soon as I arrived, I started looking for branches to hang the cotton sticks. In the pitch-black dark, I found the first one about 15–20 yards away and a few feet off the ground. I dug into my backpack and pulled out the bottle. My hands were freezing. Those cheap fabric gloves weren't doing much, and my fingers felt stiff. I dipped the cotton stick into the bottle, hung it, and repeated the process on three more branches, feeling pretty good about my first scent control setup.

All that walking had shifted my facemask, and it was bugging me. I pulled it down, and that made my face itch. Without thinking, I rubbed my hands over my face.

Instantly, I knew something was wrong.

A strong, pungent smell hit me like a brick wall. I froze and realized I'd spilled the entire bottle of doe pee into my glove while hanging the first wick. And what had I just done? I'd rubbed it all over my face. I looked down at my gloves—absolutely drenched. Then I looked at my gear—my bag, my clothes, my hat—all of which I'd touched. There was no coming back from it. I reeked.

Not only did I have to sit in that scent for the rest of the day, but my clothes and gear carried that smell for weeks. To this day, every time I see or smell doe pee, I'm instantly taken back to the time I unintentionally became the attractant. And in case you're wondering—I didn't see a single deer that day.

Scent control is one of the biggest factors in a successful hunt. You can be in the perfect spot, have the best setup, and still get busted if you don't manage your scent. The same is true in our spiritual lives. Paul writes in 2 Corinthians 2:15, "For we are to God the pleasing aroma of Christ among those who are being saved and those who are perishing." Just as scent control determines success in the woods, the "scent" of our lives—the way we speak, act, and treat others determines how people experience Christ through us.

Think about the people you encounter every day, including family, coworkers, friends, and strangers. What kind of presence do you carry into those interactions? Do people see Christ in you? Do your words encourage, uplift, and point others to Him? Or do you carry negativity, impatience, or selfishness that pushes people away? Just as hunters take precautions to eliminate unwanted odors, we should be mindful of what we allow to take root in our hearts. Are we carrying around bitterness, pride, or anger? Are we spreading gossip, stirring up division, or speaking without kindness? These things stink up our impact, just like a careless mistake in scent control ruins a hunt.

The good news is, just as we can take steps to remove our human scent before heading into the woods, we can also take steps to rid ourselves of the things that keep us from reflecting Christ. Spending time in prayer, reading God's Word, and surrounding ourselves with godly influences—these are the "scent eliminators" of our faith. They help us stay aligned with God's purpose and ensure that what we put out into the world is a pleasing aroma, not something that drives others away.

1 M.O.A.

Our lives give off a "scent" to those around us. Our words, actions, and attitudes either reflect Christ or create barriers between us and others. We should take intentional steps to remove sin, negativity, and anything that keeps us from representing Christ well. When we stay rooted in God's Word and live with purpose, we become the "pleasing aroma of Christ" to those around us.

Mission: Be intentional about the "scent" you give off to those around you. Just as hunters go to great lengths to eliminate unwanted odors in the woods, we must be just as diligent in ensuring our words, actions, and attitudes reflect Christ in everyday life.

Obedience: Take practical steps to remove negative influences and sinful habits that hinder your ability to represent Christ well. This could mean speaking with more kindness, addressing an attitude of impatience, or eliminating a habit that doesn't honor God. Actively seek to cultivate the fruits of the Spirit in your daily interactions.

Accuracy: You'll know you're on the right path when your presence in a room brings encouragement, peace, and a reflection of Christ's love. Ask yourself—are people drawn to God because of your actions, or are there things in your life that push them away? A life that carries the "pleasing aroma of Christ" leaves a lasting impact on those around you.

PRAYER

God, thank You for the reminder that my life gives off an aroma, one that either draws people closer to You or pushes them away. Help me to be intentional about the way I live, making sure that my words, actions, and heart reflect Your love and truth. When I speak, let my words encourage. When I act, let my actions reflect Your character. And when I fail, remind me of Your grace and guide me back to You. Help me be a pleasing aroma in a world that desperately needs to know You. In Jesus' name, Amen.

DAY 11
FAITH BEYOND WHAT'S SEEN

VERSE

Now faith is confidence in what we hope for and assurance about what we do not see. This is what the ancients were commended for. By faith we understand that the universe was formed at God's command, so that what is seen was not made out of what was visible.
Hebrews 11:1-3

THE TARGET

Hebrews 11:1-3 defines faith as both confidence in what we hope for and assurance in what we cannot see. This kind of faith is what sets believers apart, as it allows us to trust in God's promises even when we can't yet see the outcome. Just as the ancients were commended for their faith in God's unseen work, we too are called to believe in the unseen—the promises of God, His power, and His plan for our lives. Reflect today on how your faith shapes your perspective. Are you trusting in God's plan, even when the details are unclear?

ZEROED IN

I can't tell you how many times I've gone out into the woods and not seen a single animal. Whether it's elk hunting, deer hunting, coyote hunting, or turkey hunting, some days just feel like nothing is happening. The woods are quiet, the wind barely moves the trees, and the only thing stirring is your own thoughts. It's frustrating, especially when you've spent hours or even days scouting, prepping, and doing everything right. But the reality is, just because you don't see something doesn't mean it isn't there.

There have been plenty of mornings when I've sat for hours, barely hearing so much as a rustling leaf, only to climb down for lunch and spook deer that had been just out of sight the entire time. I've had days where nothing shows up in the morning, but by the afternoon, a shift in the wind or a distant noise sends animals moving right into my shooting lane. The woods are unpredictable, and animals are constantly adjusting their behavior based on conditions we can't always see or understand.

Maybe the deer are moving later than usual because a pack of coyotes came through during the night. Maybe your neighbor decided today was the perfect time to fire up his chainsaw, shifting all the movement in your direction. Maybe there's a hot food source just out of view, and the deer are simply feeding where you can't see them. The point is, things are happening—even when it seems like nothing is.

Hunting teaches us patience, but more than that, it teaches us trust. Trust that the effort isn't wasted. Trust that something is happening, even if it's not happening where you can see it. And most importantly, trust that when the time is right, things will come together. Sometimes that means adjusting your setup. Other times it means simply sitting still and believing that something is coming.

Our faith works the same way. Hebrews 11:1 reminds us, "Now faith is confidence in what we hope for and assurance about what we do not see." Just like in the woods, where movement happens beyond our line of sight, God is always working. There are moments in life when it feels like nothing is happening. We pray, we wait, we seek God's guidance, and yet, we see no movement. No change. No clear answer. It's easy to get discouraged, or to feel like our efforts are wasted. But just because we don't see the answer immediately doesn't mean God isn't working behind the scenes.

Think about the times in your life when you felt stuck, like nothing was happening. Then, out of nowhere, things changed. Maybe an opportunity opened up, a relationship was restored, or a situation that seemed impossible suddenly made sense. That wasn't coincidence—that was God working, preparing things in ways you couldn't see.

Isaiah 55:8-9 reminds us of this truth: "For my thoughts are not your thoughts, neither are your ways my ways," declares the Lord. "As the heavens are higher than the earth, so are my ways higher than your ways and my thoughts than your thoughts." God's timing isn't our timing. His ways aren't always what we expect. But that doesn't mean He's not moving. It means we have to trust Him even when we don't see the results immediately.

Just like in hunting, we may sit all day and not see a thing. And that's okay. Because our trust isn't in what we can see—it's in what we know to be true. God is always moving, always preparing, always working things for our good. And in our faith, we are called to do the same—waiting patiently, trusting fully, even when nothing seems to be happening.

So the next time you're sitting in the woods, wondering if anything is going to show up, remember that just because you don't see it doesn't mean it's not there. The same is true in life. Stay faithful, stay ready, and trust that in God's perfect timing, everything will come together just as it should.

1 M.O.A.

Waiting can be frustrating, whether in the woods or in life. But sometimes, the waiting is what prepares us. A quiet morning in the stand may feel unproductive, but every moment spent there increases your chances of success. In the same way, waiting on God isn't wasted time—it's an opportunity to grow in faith, trust, and preparation for what He has in store. Our job is to stay patient, remain faithful, and be ready when the moment arrives.

Mission: Strengthen your faith by trusting God's work, even when you don't see immediate results. Just like a hunter remains patient and ready even when no game is in sight, we must remain steadfast in our faith, knowing that God is always moving behind the scenes.

Obedience: Commit to daily faith-building habits. Spend time in Scripture, pray persistently even when answers seem delayed, and remind yourself of God's past faithfulness in your life. Choose to walk in obedience, even when you don't see immediate evidence of God's plan.

Accuracy: A deepened trust in God is evident when you continue to live with faith, peace, and expectation, rather than frustration and doubt. Are you patient in the waiting? Do you remain faithful in prayer and obedience even when things don't happen on your timeline? Faith isn't measured by sight—it's measured by confidence in God's promises.

PRAYER

Heavenly Father, thank You for reminding me that even when I don't see movement, You are still at work. Strengthen my faith and help me trust Your timing, even when answers don't come as quickly as I would like. Help me to remain steady, prepared, and expectant, knowing that You are always working things for my good. Teach me to let go of anxiety, frustration, and doubt, and instead, rest in the assurance of Your perfect plan. In Jesus' name, Amen.

DAY 12
BEWARE THE BEAR

VERSE

Be alert and of sober mind. Your enemy the devil prowls around like a roaring lion looking for someone to devour.
1 Peter 5:8

THE TARGET

Awareness is key in hunting. You may not see a predator, but that doesn't mean it's not there. The same is true in our spiritual lives—just because we don't see the enemy doesn't mean he isn't lurking nearby. 1 Peter 5:8 warns us to stay alert because the enemy is always looking for an opportunity to strike. The goal isn't to live in fear, but to remain spiritually aware, standing firm in faith and ready for whatever comes.

ZEROED IN

My family owns land just west of the Cascade Mountain Range in Oregon. My dad grew up in the area before moving to the Midwest, but after years away, he returned and bought more land near where he was raised. Every summer and early fall, we see elk in a section of his hazelnut orchard that we call "the bottom." This stretch of land, about 20 acres of woods and 13 acres of crops, follows a creek and always seems to draw in wildlife. Though small compared to the dense forests to the east, for months, elk show up there regularly, almost like clockwork—until, like flipping a switch, they vanish in the fall.

One year, my buddy and I decided to hunt them from a tree stand and an elevated blind my dad and I had set up in the bottom. It wasn't the most conventional approach, but with a bull elk showing up regularly on trail cameras, we figured it was worth a shot. But just before we arrived in Oregon, the farmer harvested the crops, and from that moment on, the elk disappeared from our cameras. With Plan A out the window, we turned to Plan B, heading into the foothills of the Cascades to see if we could stalk them the old-fashioned way.

I had never been in the foothills before, but my dad assured me there were no bears in that area. So, with that bit of reassurance, off we went. On the second morning of our hunt, the rain was relentless. As two guys from the Midwest, we had no idea just how thick the underbrush in the foothills would be. We parked high up on a ridge and were immediately met by an impenetrable wall of tangled vegetation. With our bows slung over our backs and rain pouring down, we pressed forward, calling for elk every so often only to be met with silence. For hours, we trudged through the underbrush, soaked to the core, battling the terrain and elements. By noon, we were exhausted, shivering, and ready to warm up. We hiked back to the truck, eager to dry off. As soon as we climbed in and shut the doors, something caught our eye—movement up ahead. Just as we started rolling forward, a bear stepped out 30 yards away, completely unfazed by our presence.

We were stunned. We had no bear spray, no deterrent, and absolutely no plan for this situation. The realization hit hard—we had just spent the entire morning unknowingly walking through its home. For a few moments, we just sat there, watching as the bear slowly wandered back into the brush. When we got back to my dad's property, I rushed inside, eager to tell him what we had seen. "You won't believe what we ran into—a bear!" I pulled up a map and pointed to the exact spot where we had been—less than a quarter mile from one of his buddy's houses. His reaction? Pure disbelief. He immediately texted his friend, and sure enough, his buddy had never seen a bear in that area either.

Awareness is everything. Whether it's in the woods or in life, the things you don't see can be just as dangerous as the things you do. In 1 Peter 5:8, we are warned: "Be alert and of sober mind. Your enemy the devil prowls around like a roaring lion looking for someone to devour." Much like how we assumed there were no bears in that area, many of us go through life assuming we're in the clear—safe from temptation, free from spiritual danger, and unbothered by the enemy's schemes. But the truth is, the enemy is always lurking. He waits for the moments when we let our guard down, when we grow complacent, when we assume we're untouchable.

That's how sin creeps in. No one wakes up one morning and suddenly decides to fall into temptation or drift away from God. It happens gradually with one small compromise at a time. A thought left unchecked. A habit left unchallenged. A temptation entertained instead of resisted. And before we realize it, we're caught in something we never saw coming. The enemy doesn't always announce his presence. Often, he works in the background, slowly shifting our focus, dulling our awareness, and making us believe we're fine... until we're not.

Staying spiritually alert requires intentional effort. Immersing yourself in God's Word is the best defense against the lies of the enemy—regular time in Scripture keeps you grounded and aware. Prayer is just as crucial; asking God for discernment allows you to recognize the spiritual battles you may not even realize you're in. Surrounding yourself with strong believers provides accountability and support, much like having a plan when navigating dangerous territory. And when warning signs appear and something feels off or your heart is being pulled in the wrong direction—take it seriously. That could be the Holy Spirit prompting you to step back and stay vigilant against unseen dangers. The reality is, we live in a spiritual world with very real battles. But as followers of Christ, we don't need to live in fear. We just need to be ready. Because the enemy? He's out there. Even when we can't see him.

1 M.O.A.

Staying alert and prepared isn't about fear, but about wisdom. When we stay rooted in God's truth, remain in prayer, and surround ourselves with fellow believers, we ensure that we are not caught off guard. Spiritual awareness is key to standing firm in our faith and resisting the traps the enemy sets.

Mission: Stay spiritually alert and prepared. Just as hunters must remain aware of their surroundings and anticipate unseen dangers, we must recognize that the enemy is always looking for an opportunity to strike. Strengthening our faith and guarding our hearts is not an option—it's a necessity.

Obedience: Take proactive steps to guard your spiritual life. Commit to daily time in Scripture to build discernment, pray for wisdom and protection, and seek accountability from strong believers who will help you stay on course. Be intentional about cutting out influences that weaken your faith.

Accuracy: Spiritual maturity is revealed by your ability to recognize and resist spiritual threats before they take hold. Are you standing firm in your faith, resisting temptation, and remaining vigilant against the enemy's tactics? A strong, prepared believer does not get caught off guard but stays rooted in God's truth.

PRAYER

Dear Jesus, thank You for the reminder that just because I don't see the enemy doesn't mean he isn't there. Help me to stay spiritually alert, to recognize the subtle ways the enemy tries to distract, discourage, or deceive me. Give me discernment to see the battles I may not even realize I'm in, and wisdom to respond with faith and courage. Keep me grounded in Your Word, anchored in prayer, and surrounded by people who strengthen my walk with You. When I'm tempted to grow complacent, wake me up. When I start to drift, draw me back. Thank You for being my refuge, my strength, and my constant defender. In Jesus' name, Amen.

DAY 13
EYES ON THE PRIZE

VERSE

I press on toward the goal to win the prize for which God has called me heavenward in Christ Jesus.
Philippians 3:14

THE TARGET

Staying focused is everything. It's easy to get distracted by obstacles, setbacks, or even the excitement of the chase, but true success comes from staying locked in on the goal. Philippians 3:14 urges us to press on toward the ultimate prize—our calling in Christ. When we fix our eyes on Him, rather than being pulled away by distractions, frustrations, or temporary pursuits, we move forward with purpose. Today is about focus, perseverance, and making sure we're chasing after what truly matters. Are you keeping your eyes on the prize, or have distractions pulled you off course?

ZEROED IN

Every year, there's always that one buck or maybe two that steals the attention of every hunter in the area. The one with the perfect rack, incredible mass, or maybe even a unique feature like a droptine or a split brow tine. For most of us, having an entire hit list of giant bucks like the guys on TV would be the dream, but in reality, most seasons are spent chasing after just one or two. That's the deer we think about when setting stands, checking trail cams, and driving to the farm. And sometimes, despite all our preparation, we go the entire season without ever laying eyes on them.

I've definitely had my fair share of monster target bucks over the years. One year in particular, I had two incredible deer show up on camera. One was a 14-pointer, and the other was a nice 10-pointer with an additional droptine. I still have an awesome picture of them standing side by side in full velvet—one of those trail cam shots that makes you stare at your phone a little too long. They were the kind of bucks that made you rethink every stand placement, reconsider every wind direction, and maybe even whisper a quick prayer asking for a little divine favor.

But despite all my efforts, I never harvested either of them. In fact, I never even laid eyes on the 14-pointer. I sat in my stand for countless hours, playing mental chess with a deer that had no clue how obsessed I was with him. And while I never got the chance to take a shot, knowing they were out there kept me motivated every single time I climbed into the stand. Every hunt felt like it could be the one. Because that's the thing about chasing a target buck—you don't lose focus just because you haven't seen him yet. You keep showing up, staying ready, and believing that the moment will come. And if needed, you adjust your strategy, discipline yourself to wait for the right opportunity, and refuse to settle for anything less than the prize you've set your sights on.

What if we had that same passion for God? Our ultimate goal as followers of Christ isn't just to go through the motions of faith; it's to fix our eyes on eternity and press toward the greatest reward of all, being with God in heaven. Philippians 3:20 reminds us, "But our citizenship is in heaven. And we eagerly await a Savior from there, the Lord Jesus Christ." Heaven isn't just some distant, abstract idea—it's our true home. The place where every tear is wiped away, where sin and suffering no longer exist, and where we will experience the fullness of joy in God's presence.

Just like chasing after a specific buck takes commitment and effort, so does keeping our hearts set on the things of God. There are so many distractions in this world that can pull us away from our true purpose. It's easy to get caught up in temporary pleasures, personal ambitions, or even just the daily grind of life. But Jesus calls us to something greater. He reminds us in Luke 12:34, "For where your treasure is, there your heart will be also." Our hearts are often drawn to what we value most, and if we're not careful, we can place more importance on the fleeting things of this world than on the eternal things of God. Everything we chase after on earth, such as success, wealth, recognition, and target bucks, will eventually fade away. But the pursuit of Christ and the promise of eternity with Him will never lose its value. The difference between hunting and our faith is that with hunting, even if you don't get that buck, it's not the end of the world. But if we miss our true target, if we get so caught up in earthly things that we lose sight of God, we risk missing out on the ultimate prize.

So what are you truly aiming for in your life? Are you focused on things that will last forever, or are you distracted by the temporary? Just like in hunting, where we discipline ourselves to wait for the right buck, we must train our hearts to stay focused on what really matters. The reward is far greater than any trophy buck—it's eternity with Christ. That's the goal worth everything.

1 M.O.A.

Our ultimate reward isn't something temporary or material—it's the promise of eternal life with God in heaven. Success, comfort, and even everyday responsibilities can take priority if we're not careful. Staying committed to our faith requires intentional effort, discipline, and a constant realignment of our hearts toward God's greater purpose. When we keep our eyes fixed on Him, we find true fulfillment that lasts beyond this life.

Mission: Keep your focus on the ultimate goal of eternity with Christ. Just as hunters fix their sights on a target buck, we are called to set our minds on things above, not on the temporary distractions of this world. Stay committed to pursuing God's purpose for your life.

Obedience: Align your daily choices with your heavenly goal. Prioritize your relationship with Christ by dedicating specific time to prayer, reading Scripture, and living in obedience to His calling. Be intentional about removing distractions that pull you away from your faith.

Accuracy: Evaluate what you're chasing. Are your goals and desires leading you closer to Christ, or are they focused on temporary things that will fade away? Ask God to help you stay focused on what truly matters and to shape your heart to desire Him above all else.

PRAYER

Lord, thank You for reminding me that my ultimate prize isn't found in this world but in eternity with You. It's so easy to get caught up in the distractions, pressures, and temporary rewards of life. Help me to fix my eyes on You and to pursue the things that truly matter. Give me wisdom to recognize when I'm chasing after things that won't last and the discipline to realign my heart with Your purpose. Strengthen my faith, deepen my desire to know You more, and keep me focused on the promise of heaven. Let my actions, words, and choices reflect a life that is lived for Your glory. In Jesus' name, Amen.

DAY 14
WEATHERING THE STORM

VERSE

Consider it pure joy, my brothers and sisters, whenever you face trials of many kinds, because you know that the testing of your faith produces perseverance. Let perseverance finish its work so that you may be mature and complete, not lacking anything.
James 1:2-4

THE TARGET

Trials are not just obstacles; they are opportunities to grow. They develop perseverance, shaping us into who God has called us to be. Difficulties may come when we least expect them, but they are not without purpose. God uses every challenge to strengthen our faith, refine our character, and prepare us for what's ahead. The question isn't whether hardships will come—they will. The real question is how we will respond. Will we trust that God is using every challenge to strengthen us, or will we allow difficulties to shake our faith?

ZEROED IN

Rain is something every outdoorsman relies on. It fills the rivers, greens the fields, and keeps the woods alive. But while it's essential, it's rarely enjoyable in the moment. When it shows up at the wrong time, it can turn a perfectly planned day into a cold, soggy mess. Most of the time, we head for cover and try to stay dry. And when we do tough it out, we're often left soaked, shivering, and questioning whether it was worth it. Still, some of my best hunts have happened in steady rain—like the time it poured for three straight days and the deer never stopped moving. Other times, rain brings silence. The woods feel empty, and hours pass without a single sign of life. In the outdoors, weather is unpredictable. Rain might kickstart activity one day and bring everything to a halt the next.

One of my favorite fish to target is walleye on the Great Lakes. Maybe it's because of how I grew up fishing, but there's something special about reeling in a big, 30-inch walleye. They look cool, they put up a decent fight, and on a good day, they're usually pretty easy to catch. Unless, of course, a massive storm rolls in.

One summer, we planned a single-day fishing trip to Lake Erie. We had just one shot at getting on the water—between everyone's schedules, there was no backup plan. We arrived the night before, excited and ready to go, until we saw a flash of lightning light up the sky, followed by a deep, rolling crack of thunder. We all looked at each other and immediately pulled up the radar. The forecast showed the storm was supposed to clear up by 7 a.m., so we figured we'd still be able to make the most of our trip. But it didn't just rain—it stormed all night. The worst of it hit around 3 or 4 a.m., with winds howling against the windows and rain hammering the roof so hard it sounded like gravel hitting the cabin. Every time I woke up, the storm was still raging, making me wonder if we'd even get on the water.

By morning, the sky was clear, but the lake had already taken the hit. When we got to the marina, we met up with our charter guide, Mike—a guy we had trusted for years. He glanced at the lake, then back at us, hesitant. "I don't know, guys," he finally said. "After a storm like that, today is gonna be rough." Now, when Mike says he isn't sure about a day, he means it. He's taken us out plenty of times before, and he's always put us on the fish. If he was doubting the trip, we knew the odds weren't in our favor. He gave us the option to reschedule, but knowing that wasn't really possible with our schedules, we decided to give it a shot anyway.

Five hours later, I was the only one to land a walleye—and it was no trophy. We could see the fish. The sonar lit up with massive marks below us, proof that we were in the right spot. But no matter what we tried, they wouldn't bite. We changed depths, swapped lures, adjusted speeds—nothing worked. Finally, after hours on the water, we called it early and headed back in, knowing that no amount of effort was going to change the conditions.

That day on the lake reminded me of something simple but important. No matter how much we prepare, some things remain outside of our control. We can have the right guide, the best gear, and be in the perfect location, but if the conditions aren't right, we can't force the outcome. In life, we often experience the same thing. We work hard, make plans, and do everything in our power to ensure success, only to find that things don't go the way we hoped. But that doesn't mean our effort was wasted. It means we have to trust that God's timing and purpose are bigger than our own.

Life is full of unexpected storms. Sometimes, they roll in with warning, and other times, they catch us completely off guard. We can prepare, strategize, and do everything in our power to control the outcome, but in the end, some things are simply out of our hands. And while storms are rarely enjoyable in the moment, they often serve a greater purpose than we realize.

In the midst of those storms, it can be hard to see the purpose. Trials rarely feel like a blessing when we're facing them head-on. But James 1:2-4 challenges us to shift our perspective. Hardships stretch us, build endurance, and develop perseverance that strengthens our faith. Just as storms bring much-needed rain to the land, struggles in life shape us in ways we may not recognize at first. We often want struggles to pass quickly, but sometimes, God allows them to do their work by refining us, growing us, and shifting our focus toward Him.

Looking back, there have been times when life didn't go as planned. Maybe you've faced disappointment, discouragement, or a season of uncertainty. At the time, it may have felt frustrating or unfair, but now, can you see how God used it for something greater? Maybe He strengthened your faith. Maybe He closed a door to open a better one. Maybe He revealed something about Himself that you wouldn't have seen otherwise. We don't always understand what God is doing in the moment, but we can trust that no trial is wasted.

Just like the storm that changed the conditions of the lake, the trials we walk through change the condition of our hearts—but for the better. They teach us endurance. They strip away self-reliance and deepen our trust in God. The next time a storm rolls in, whether it's a setback, an unexpected challenge, or a season of waiting, remember that it's not a sign of failure but an opportunity for transformation. Stand firm in faith, knowing that every trial is molding you for a purpose greater than you can imagine.

1 M.O.A.

Storms in life aren't just obstacles—they are opportunities for growth. Our response to them matters. Instead of resisting or wishing them away, trust that God is using every hardship for something greater. When challenges arise, lean into them with faith, knowing they are shaping you for God's higher purpose.

Mission: Learn to see challenges as opportunities for growth rather than obstacles to avoid. Instead of focusing on the difficulty of your current struggle, shift your mindset to recognize how God may be using it to strengthen and prepare you for what's ahead.

Obedience: When difficulties arise, choose to rely on God's strength instead of your own. Turn to Him for guidance and peace or seek counsel from fellow believers. Make it a practice to trust in His wisdom, knowing that He is with you through every challenge, shaping you for what lies ahead.

Accuracy: Assess your response to trials. Are you growing in endurance, faith, and trust in God through difficulties, or are you becoming discouraged and distant from Him? Ask God to help you recognize His work in your struggles and trust that He is leading you toward something greater.

PRAYER

Dear Jesus, thank You for reminding me that every storm has a purpose. I may not always understand why challenges come my way, but I trust that You are using them to shape me, strengthen me, and draw me closer to You. When life doesn't go as planned, help me to respond with faith instead of frustration. Teach me to lean on You instead of my own understanding, and help me to see trials not as setbacks, but as opportunities to grow. Thank You for being my shelter in the storm and my strength in every season. In Jesus' name, Amen.

DAY 15
AIMING FOR GRACE

VERSE

But he said to me, 'My grace is sufficient for you, for my power is made perfect in weakness.' Therefore I will boast all the more gladly about my weaknesses, so that Christ's power may rest on me.
2 Corinthians 12:9

THE TARGET

Paul embraces the paradox that God's grace is most powerful when we are weakest. It's in our moments of vulnerability and struggle that God's strength is most evident. This verse challenges us to shift our perspective. Rather than hiding or resenting our weaknesses, we are called to boast in them, knowing that they are the very spaces where God's power can shine through. Today, reflect on how you can allow God's grace to shine through your own weaknesses. Instead of relying on your own strength, trust that His power is more than enough to carry you through.

ZEROED IN

Remember back on Day 1, when I forgot my orange hat on opening morning? Well, the story doesn't stop there. Feeling pretty good about myself for securing a last-minute replacement, I was optimistic about the morning. As first light broke, the distant crack of gunshots echoed across the woods. Deer were on the move.

That morning, I was hunting on the ground near a water source, tucked into some thick brush that was almost as high as my body. The wind was blowing perfectly straight into my face, and I was set up right where the deer normally traveled. About twenty minutes after legal shooting time, I spotted two does heading directly toward me. Minutes passed, and before I knew it, they were just fifteen yards away. Normally by now, I would have already taken the shot, but the brush was so thick that I decided to wait for a clearer opening. They kept moving closer. Then, out of nowhere, one of them finally stepped into a tiny clearing just five yards away—and bolted. No warning, no reason, just gone. I couldn't get her to stop, and both deer disappeared into the woods.

I was frustrated, but I still had hope for the morning. The deer were moving, and I knew I might get another shot. Sure enough, around 9:30, I caught movement to my right. Another deer was walking parallel to me. Without thinking, I smoothly swiveled to my right, still covered by the brush, and let out a bleat to stop it. Sure enough, it froze perfectly broadside at fifty yards. It was a textbook shot. I settled my aim, squeezed the trigger, and watched as the deer took off. It wasn't wounded. It was jumping away like it had just been mildly inconvenienced. I knew I had missed. But how?

I had chosen to use my shotgun that day because of the thick cover I knew I'd sit in. It had fiber optic sights and had been zeroed at fifty yards just a week prior. I was confident in it. Yet, I had completely whiffed. I checked my gun, running my hand over the barrel and stock, trying to figure out what went wrong. Then I noticed it—the rear sight was loose. Not just a little off, but completely detached from where it should have been. My elevation screw was gone. I had no chance of making an accurate shot.

As I walked back to the truck, that familiar frustration started creeping in. The voice that says, "You should've checked your gear. You should've done better. You blew it." And maybe I could've done a few things differently. But in that moment, I knew I had a choice—keep beating myself up, or give myself a little grace. Not to excuse the miss, but to remember that failure happens, even when we've done everything right. That's part of hunting, and it's part of life.

No one likes to fail. Whether it's missing a shot on a deer, falling short in your career, or making a mistake in your personal life, failure is frustrating. You prepare, you practice, you do everything in your power to succeed—yet sometimes, despite your best efforts, things don't go as planned.

2 Corinthians 12:9 reminds us that God's grace isn't just enough—it's where His power is made perfect. Paul understood what it meant to struggle with weakness, but instead of seeing it as a limitation, he saw it as a place for God to work. The truth is, our failures don't push God away. Instead, they create an opportunity for Him to draw us closer, reminding us that our strength was never the key to success—His was. That means your failures do not define you—God's grace does.

Yet, how often do we believe the opposite? We convince ourselves that our mistakes make us less valuable, that we need to prove ourselves, or that God must be disappointed in us when we fall short. But that's not how grace works. God doesn't love you because you're perfect. He loves you because you're His. Even when we miss the mark, He doesn't walk away. Grace steps in where we can't measure up.

But grace isn't just about covering our mistakes, it's about transformation. When Peter denied Jesus three times, he must have felt like his failure was too great to come back from. Yet Jesus met him in that very place, restored him, and gave him an even greater purpose. God's grace doesn't erase our past, but rather it redeems it. It shapes us, humbles us, and reminds us that our worth isn't in our performance but in His love for us.

So what do we do when we fall short? Take responsibility. Grace doesn't mean ignoring our mistakes. It means acknowledging them and allowing God to use them for growth. Second, we refuse to let failure define us. Missing a shot doesn't make you a bad hunter, and failing in life doesn't mean you're beyond redemption. God's grace is bigger than any mistake you've made. Finally, we press on. Just like in hunting, you learn from what went wrong, make adjustments, and get back out there. God doesn't want you stuck in your past—He wants you to keep moving forward in His grace.

That day in the woods, I missed my shot—but that didn't mean I was a bad hunter. It didn't mean I was a failure. It simply meant there was something to learn. The same is true in life. Our failures aren't the end of the story; they're opportunities for God to step in with His grace.

If you've been carrying the weight of failure, it's time to let it go. God's grace is sufficient. It always has been. It always will be. Your mistakes do not define you—He does.

1 M.O.A.

Failure is part of the journey, but it doesn't have to define you. Whether in the woods or in life, missed opportunities and mistakes are part of the process. The good news? God's grace is greater than our failures. His power is made perfect in our weakness, and He uses every shortcoming to shape us into who He's calling us to be. Instead of letting failure hold you back, use it as a stepping stone toward growth and deeper trust in Him.

Mission: To embrace God's grace in our failures, understanding that our mistakes do not define us—God's redemption does. Instead of being weighed down by past failures, we should seek growth and allow God to use them for our good.

Obedience: When you fall short, choose to respond with faith rather than self-condemnation. Confess your struggles to God, lean on His grace, and commit to learning from the experience rather than letting it hold you back. Find a specific Scripture that speaks to God's strength in our weakness, and use it as a daily reminder of His power.

Accuracy: Success is measured by how we move forward. Are you dwelling on failure, or are you allowing God to use it for transformation? Take a step today toward growth—whether it's seeking accountability, making amends, or shifting your perspective to align with God's truth.

PRAYER

Heavenly Father, thank You for Your grace that covers all my mistakes and missed chances. When I fall short and things don't go as planned, remind me that Your strength shines through my weakness. Help me see failures as chances to grow, not as measures of my worth. Give me the humility to accept correction and the courage to keep going, trusting that Your plan is always bigger than my mistakes. Help me lean on You, knowing that every setback leads to a future full of hope. Let Your grace transform me in every struggle. In Jesus' name, Amen.

DAY 16
ENTRUSTED, NOT OWNED

VERSE

Whoever can be trusted with very little can also be trusted with much, and whoever is dishonest with very little will also be dishonest with much.
Luke 16:10

THE TARGET

God isn't just concerned with the big moments in our lives. He sees the small, everyday choices we make when no one is watching. Are we honest in the little things? Do we respect what belongs to others? Do we manage what we have well, even when it doesn't seem like much? Luke 16:10 explains that faithfulness in the small things prepares us for greater responsibility. Stewardship isn't about ownership—it's about responsibility. The way we handle what isn't ours reveals our character and determines whether we can be entrusted with more. God calls us to be faithful with what we've been given, not just when the stakes are high, but in every aspect of our lives.

ZEROED IN

Hunting access is a privilege, not a right. My hunting experiences wouldn't be the same without the generosity of landowners who have allowed me onto their property. Whether it was a prime deer hunting spot, a field for coyote hunting, or a pond to fish, I've always relied on the trust and kindness of others. And when someone grants you that kind of access, it comes with an expectation—you respect the land, follow the rules, and leave it better than you found it.

I've always taken that responsibility seriously. I close every gate that I open, pick up trash even if it's not mine, and never cut corners. Over the years, I've seen firsthand how being a good steward leads to greater opportunities. I've had landowners start me off with access to just a small section of their property, only to later open up more land as they saw I was trustworthy. What began as a handshake agreement for a single field turned into permission to hunt the entire farm because I demonstrated that I was responsible.

But I've also seen what happens when people take that privilege for granted. Some hunters have lost access to incredible properties by ignoring boundaries, leaving trash behind, or disregarding the landowner's rules. One careless mistake, one poor decision, and the opportunity is gone. I've heard stories of landowners revoking access because someone cut down a tree without permission, hunted game they weren't authorized to pursue, or left a gate open, allowing livestock to escape. A single act of negligence doesn't just cost you the chance to return—it damages the reputation of hunters as a whole.

There was one particular farm where I had permission to hunt deer, but from day one, it was clear that trust had to be earned. The landowner had allowed others access before, only to have them show up unannounced, damage his fields, or ignore his rules. Understandably, he was cautious about letting anyone new onto his land. But I was determined to prove I was different. I kept my word, texted him each time I arrived and left, and helped with small projects around the farm whenever possible. By the end of the season, he told me I was welcome back anytime. Respect and responsibility built trust, and that trust led to greater opportunity.

Hunting access is earned, and in many ways, the same principle applies to life. How we handle what isn't ours reveals our character. Whether it's land, resources, relationships, time, or responsibilities—everything we have is a gift from God, entrusted to us for a purpose. God watches how we manage what we've been given before entrusting us with more.

Jesus made it clear that faithfulness in small things leads to greater responsibility. If we aren't trusted with the little things, why would we be entrusted with more? Faithfulness isn't about grand gestures—it's about the everyday choices, the quiet decisions no one else sees. Small compromises may seem harmless, but just like a careless hunter can lose access to great land, neglecting the small things can close doors we didn't realize were even open.

Think about the areas in your life where you've been entrusted with something. Are you stewarding your finances wisely, treating your relationships with care, and working diligently, or simply getting by? God's blessings and opportunities are privileges, not guarantees. Honoring commitments, keeping our word, and being trustworthy—even when no one is watching—is true stewardship. Trust isn't built in a day, but it can be lost in a moment.

God isn't waiting for perfection, but He is looking for faithfulness. He sees how we handle what He's given us—not to take it away, but to prepare us for even greater things. If we want more—whether in relationships, opportunities, influence, or blessings—we must first prove ourselves faithful with what we have now. Are you being a good steward of what God has placed in your hands? Ask yourself that often—because faithfulness in the small things positions us for greater things ahead.

> **1 M.O.A.**
> Faithfulness is revealed in the small things. It's not about how much we have but how well we manage what has been placed in our hands. Whether it's land, time, relationships, or responsibilities, every resource we've been given is an opportunity to demonstrate integrity and wisdom. If we want to experience more of God's blessings, influence, and opportunities, we must first prove that we can handle what He has already placed in our care.

> **Mission:** To be faithful stewards of what has been entrusted to us, recognizing that everything we have is a gift from God. Whether it's land, relationships, resources, or responsibilities, we are called to manage them with integrity and honor.
>
> **Obedience:** Commit to demonstrating faithfulness in both small and significant responsibilities. Show gratitude to those who trust you, take care of what you've been given, and make intentional choices that reflect responsibility and respect.
>
> **Accuracy:** Success is measured by consistency in stewardship. If more were entrusted to you tomorrow, would you be ready? Evaluate whether your actions align with the kind of character that leads to greater opportunities.

PRAYER

Lord, thank You for entrusting me with the opportunities, relationships, and resources in my life. I know that nothing I have is truly mine, and it all belongs to You. Help me to be a faithful steward of what You've given me, whether it seems big or small. Give me wisdom to handle responsibilities with integrity, diligence to honor my commitments, and a heart that values what You've placed in my care. When I'm tempted to cut corners or take things for granted, remind me that faithfulness in the little things prepares me for the greater things You have in store. Let my actions reflect Your goodness, and may the way I manage what I've been given bring glory to You. In Jesus' name, Amen.

DAY 17
SOMETIMES WE STUMBLE

VERSE

The Lord makes firm the steps of the one who delights in him; though he may stumble, he will not fall, for the Lord upholds him with his hand.
Psalm 37:23-24

THE TARGET

At some point, we all stumble. Sometimes it's a small misstep, an embarrassing moment, or a lesson learned the hard way. Other times, it feels like a complete wipeout, leaving us questioning how we'll recover. Psalm 37:23-24 assures us that even when we stumble, we are not abandoned. God holds us up with His hand, guiding our steps and steadying us when we fall. The Christian walk is all about perseverance. Trusting that when we lose our footing, God is still in control. Today, think about how you respond when you stumble. Do you let failure define you, or do you allow God to use it to strengthen your faith?

ZEROED IN

My buddy Dave and I decided we wanted to go on a small weekend fly-fishing getaway. Neither of us had ever fly-fished before, but we were eager to try something different. Through a mutual connection, we got in touch with a guide in Virginia who agreed to show us the ropes.

We left early in the morning and made it to Virginia by dinnertime, excited for the adventure ahead. The next morning, we met our guide in a hay pasture nestled in the mountains. The rolling fields had just been cut, leaving a vibrant green hue across the open land. It was one of those picture-perfect moments—cool mountain air, the scent of fresh hay, and the sound of a nearby stream trickling over the rocks. This is where we spent the first hour learning the basics of fly fishing. Casting felt awkward at first, but after some practice, we started getting the hang of it.

Once we felt somewhat competent, we headed down to the creek bordering the pasture to put our new skills to the test. The only problem? Nothing was biting. Not even a nibble. After an hour of watching our flies drift aimlessly down the water, we decided to move to another spot.

That turned out to be the right call. Within minutes of arriving at the new location, we were reeling in rainbow trout left and right. They weren't monsters by any means, but we didn't care—we were actually doing it! We fished for a couple of hours, catching and releasing, enjoying the rhythm of the cast and the rush of the fight.

After a quick break for lunch, we decided to switch things up and head to a different river. The story started the same—slow at first—but after wading upstream, we found a promising section of water. The problem was, we needed to go up on the bank and walk for a bit because the water in that stretch was too deep to wade through.

So there we were, trudging through a cow pasture about ten feet above the river, fly rods in hand, feeling like we were on some grand expedition. Finally, we found a good spot to climb back into the water. The bank had a bit of a drop—about five feet down to a ledge, then another five feet into the water itself. Our guide went first, stepping carefully down into the river before taking off upstream.

As I followed, my foot caught on something, and before I knew it, I was stumbling forward into the stream. I flailed for a second before regaining my footing just in time to hear Dave burst out laughing. "You're not supposed to fall in!" he said, full of sarcasm, clearly enjoying my near wipeout.

I turned around, ready to fire back a response, when suddenly—Dave's foot snagged on a root. And in the most glorious moment of poetic justice I've ever witnessed, he was going down. Hard. It was slow motion. One second, he was laughing at me, and the next, he was midair, arms wide open, heading straight for the water. And not just any water—this was a four-foot-deep section, and he landed in full belly-flop form. He disappeared beneath the surface, his entire body submerged under water.

When he finally emerged, gasping for air, his expression was a mix of shock, disbelief, and pure regret. I, on the other hand, was doubled over, crying from laughter. I'm talking about the kind of laugh that makes your ribs hurt. The kind of laugh that makes you weak in the knees. The kind of laugh that gets even funnier when the other person is not amused.

After catching his breath, even Dave had to admit—it was hilarious. Soaking wet and dripping, he shook his head, grinned, and kept on fishing. Because what else can you do? Sometimes, you just have to laugh, shake it off, and keep going.

In life, we all stumble. Sometimes, it's in the literal sense—like Dave taking an unexpected plunge into the river. But more often, it's in our decisions, our struggles, and our failures. No matter how much we prepare, no matter how carefully we plan our steps, there will be moments when we trip, fall, and find ourselves gasping for air.

Psalm 37:23-24 tells us that though we may stumble, we will not be utterly cast down because the Lord upholds us with His hand. That's a promise. God doesn't prevent us from stumbling, but He does promise to catch us when we do. The question is—how do we respond when we fall? Do we let embarrassment, frustration, or guilt keep us down? Or do we get back up, shake off the failure, and keep moving forward?

Too often, we let our mistakes define us. We replay our failures over and over in our minds, letting them weigh us down and convince us we're not good enough. But God doesn't define us by our worst moments—He defines us by His grace.

Falling short doesn't mean we've failed permanently. It means we have an opportunity to grow. Think about Peter walking on water. He had the faith to step out of the boat, but when he took his eyes off Jesus, he started to sink. Even then, Jesus didn't let him go. He reached out, lifted Peter up, and walked with him through the waves.

Maybe you've had moments where you've stumbled spiritually, emotionally, or even morally. Maybe you've made decisions you regret. Maybe you've fallen into patterns of sin, discouragement, or fear. But stumbling doesn't mean you're finished. God's grace is greater than any fall, and His hand is always there to lift you back up.

So the next time you stumble, don't stay down. Own it, learn from it, and keep moving forward. Just like Dave didn't let a soaking-wet fall ruin his day, don't let your failures keep you from pursuing what God has for you. He's not done with you yet.

Get up, shake it off, and keep fishing.

1 M.O.A.
Stumbling is inevitable, but it's not the end of the story. Every time we fall—whether in life, faith, or even out on the river—we have a choice. Will we let failure define us, or will we learn from it and let it shape us into who God is calling us to become? Our growth isn't measured by how many times we avoid falling, but by how we respond when we do. God's grace doesn't remove the struggle, but it strengthens us to get back up.

Mission: Keep moving forward. The goal is perseverance. When you stumble, don't let shame or discouragement hold you back. Instead, recognize the opportunity to learn, grow, and deepen your faith through the process.

Obedience: Instead of hiding mistakes or letting them discourage you, bring them before God. Ask Him what He wants you to learn from them. Surround yourself with godly influences who will encourage and challenge you, and commit to a specific step—whether it's seeking accountability, memorizing a verse

> to remind you of His grace, or stepping out in faith despite past failures.
>
> **Accuracy:** How you respond to stumbling is what matters most. You'll know you're making progress when you recover quicker, trust God deeper, and allow struggles to strengthen your faith rather than shake it. A strong faith isn't one that never falls—it's one that keeps standing back up.

PRAYER

Heavenly Father, thank You for walking with me even when I stumble. I know that in life, just like in the woods or on the water, there will be moments when I lose my footing. I'll trip, I'll fall, and I'll make mistakes. But Lord, I am so grateful that I am never beyond Your grace. When I falter, remind me that I am not defined by my failures but by Your love. Teach me to get back up, to learn from my missteps, and to trust that You are using every fall to strengthen my faith. Thank You for Your faithfulness, Your grace, and Your unshakable presence in my life. In Jesus' name, Amen.

DAY 18
MORE THAN THE RUT

VERSE

There is a time for everything, and a season for every activity under the heavens.
Ecclesiastes 3:1

THE TARGET

Life is made up of seasons, each with its own purpose, challenges, and blessings. Ecclesiastes 3:1 reminds us that there is a time for everything, and wisdom comes in recognizing which season we are in. There are times to work hard and times to rest, times to pursue our goals and times to invest in relationships. When we align our priorities with God's timing, we find peace instead of pressure, purpose instead of frustration. Today, take a step back and ask yourself: Are you embracing the season God has placed you in, or are you resisting it?

ZEROED IN

Now that I'm a dad, autumn looks a little different. I'm not disappearing into the woods every weekend from sunup to sundown like I used to. These days, my hunting trips are fewer—maybe two to four times a month—and I'm usually home by the afternoon. And while hunting has always been my therapy, an escape from the busyness of life, I've realized something even more important. I don't want to miss out on time with my little ones.

Each year, as the rut kicks into full swing, another important event rolls around—Trunk or Treat, the Halloween event our local church puts on. Taking our girls to gather candy from the decorated trunks has become a tradition. Of course, it always seems to land on a Saturday afternoon, right when I know the deer are moving. And sure enough, as I scroll through my trail camera pictures later that night, there he is—my target buck—standing broadside at 20 yards, practically smirking at me.

The younger version of me would have agonized over that missed opportunity. I would've thought about how, if I had just been in the stand, that could have been my moment. But the older I get, the more I realize that some moments are far more important than a trophy on the wall. My daughter won't remember whether or not I tagged a big buck that year, but she will remember if I was there—lifting her up so she could reach into a dinosaur-themed trunk for candy, laughing with her, making memories.

Seasons of life change. There was a time when hunting was my top priority every fall. I planned everything around it. But now, I'm in a different season—one where being present as a father takes precedence. That doesn't mean I don't still love hunting, but it does mean I've learned that not every season is meant to be about me.

In Ecclesiastes 3, we read that there is a time for everything and a season for every activity. This teaches us to embrace the season we're in, rather than resisting it, recognizing that each moment has its own purpose.

Too often, we get caught up in chasing what we think we should be doing, and we miss what God has placed right in front of us. Maybe you're in a season where you're grinding at work, pushing yourself harder than ever. Or maybe you're in a season where you need to slow down, spend time with your family, and focus on what matters most. The challenge is recognizing that just because one season was right for us in the past doesn't mean it's the season we're meant to live in forever.

Hunting illustrates this principle perfectly. There's a season for preparation, a season for patience, and a season for action. A hunter doesn't rush the process—scouting, setting stands, and waiting for the right moment are all part of the pursuit. Success comes when we recognize the importance of timing and adapt to the conditions. But when we try to force something to happen before it's time or refuse to adjust, we only end up frustrated. The same applies to life. If we're constantly fighting the season we're in—wishing we were somewhere else, doing something else—we'll miss the blessings right in front of us.

Think about where you are right now. Are you embracing this season, or are you frustrated because it doesn't look like the last one? Are you chasing things that won't matter in the long run, or are you investing in what lasts—your faith, your family, and the people God has placed in your life?

Hunting will always be there. The rut comes every year. But some opportunities, some moments, won't. Being present, being engaged in the season we're in—that's what truly matters. So if you ever find yourself sitting in a parking lot full of decorated trunks and costumed kids, instead of in your treestand, know this—you're right where you're supposed to be.

1 M.O.A.

Seasons change, and with them, our priorities must shift. There is a time for striving and a time for resting, a time for pursuing our goals and a time for investing in what matters most. When we align our lives with God's timing, we find peace, purpose, and fulfillment. Not in always doing more, but in being faithful with where He has placed us.

Mission: Recognize the importance of seasons in your life. Instead of resisting the moments that pull you away from personal pursuits, embrace the time God has given you to invest in your family, relationships, and responsibilities. Prioritize what truly matters, knowing that each season has a purpose.

Obedience: This week, be intentional about stepping away from distractions and fully engaging in the season you're in. Whether it's spending uninterrupted time with family, putting work aside to rest, or shifting your focus to something outside of your usual routine, trust that honoring God's timing will bring lasting rewards.

Accuracy: Rather than feeling constantly pulled in different directions, you embrace where you are with confidence, trusting that being present in the moment is just as important as pursuing future goals. When your choices align with God's timing, you experience fulfillment, knowing that what matters most is not just what you achieve, but how you invest in the people and purpose He has given you.

PRAYER

Lord, thank You for the reminder that there is a time for everything and that Your timing is always perfect. Help me to embrace the season I'm in, not rushing ahead or looking back with regret, but fully present in the moments that matter most. Give me wisdom to balance my passions and responsibilities, knowing that my greatest calling is to love and serve those You have placed in my life. When I feel the pull to chase after my own desires, remind me that true fulfillment comes from following Your plan. Teach me to trust that when I honor You with my time, You will bless each season and make everything beautiful in its time. In Jesus' name, Amen.

DAY 19
WORTH THE WAIT

VERSE

But our citizenship is in heaven. And we eagerly await a Savior from there, the Lord Jesus Christ, who, by the power that enables him to bring everything under his control, will transform our lowly bodies so that they will be like his glorious body.
Philippians 3:20-21

THE TARGET

Waiting isn't easy, but the best things in life are always worth it. As hunters, we anticipate the peak of the season—the moment when everything we've prepared for finally comes together. In the same way, as believers, we are waiting for something far greater, the promise of eternity with Christ. Philippians 3:20 reminds us that our true citizenship is in heaven, and we eagerly await our Savior's return. No matter how good life gets, the best is still ahead. The struggles, waiting, and preparation we go through now are leading to something beyond anything we can imagine. The question is, are we living with that perspective? Are we setting our hearts on what's temporary, or are we eagerly waiting for what is to come?

ZEROED IN

There's no time like the rut. After months of preparation, patience, discipline, and trunk or treating, the prime days finally arrive. Everything changes, and bucks that were nocturnal start moving in daylight, new deer show up out of nowhere, and opportunities that didn't exist a week ago suddenly appear.

This is what we've been waiting for. This is why we put in the early mornings, the hours of scouting, the time spent fine-tuning our setups. And when the conditions line up perfectly, when the adrenaline kicks in, and when everything finally comes together—it makes every bit of effort worth it.

But what makes this part of the season so special? It's not just the action; it's the anticipation. The build-up. The waiting. The fact that we had to put in the work, be patient, and trust that the right moment would come. And when it finally does, it's more rewarding than we ever could have imagined.

Ask any hunter about the rut, and you'll hear the same thing—you don't want to miss it. If there's ever a time to be in the woods, this is it. The stakes are high, and the excitement is even higher. We also know the rut doesn't last forever. It's a short window of time, and if we're not ready for it, we miss out. That feeling—that expectation that the best is just ahead—is a glimpse of something even greater. As incredible as these moments in the woods are, they're just a shadow of what's to come. Because beyond this life, something far better is waiting.

As much as we look forward to these days in the woods, they don't compare to what's ahead. Philippians 3:20 says that our true citizenship isn't here—it's in heaven. And just like we wait all year for the best days of hunting, we are waiting for something even greater—the day we step into eternity with Christ.

But waiting isn't always easy. We live in a world that chases instant gratification. We want results now, success now, fulfillment now. The idea of waiting and trusting that something better is coming goes against everything culture tells us. Yet some of the greatest things in life require patience and preparation.

Hunting teaches us that. We don't expect success overnight. We put in the work. We trust the process. We don't get discouraged when the action is slow because we know something good is coming. And when the time comes, the waiting makes the reward even sweeter. The same is true in our faith.

But the reality is that many people live as if this world is all there is. They plan, prepare, and pursue things that only last for a moment, forgetting that eternity is ahead. Jesus warns us in Matthew 6:19-20 not to store up treasures on earth, where they fade and disappear, but to store up treasures in heaven. The rut is exciting, but it comes and goes. The things we chase in life—success, wealth, recognition—will one day fade, too. But heaven? That's forever. That's where our real treasure is.

Are we living like people who know the best is still ahead?

Think about the anticipation you feel leading up to the rut. The preparation. The expectation. The readiness. Do you live with that same level of anticipation for eternity? Do you wake up each day with the mindset that something greater is coming, that this world is temporary, and that heaven is worth living for? Or are you too caught up in the here and now to even think about it?

The rut is worth waiting for, but eternity is worth even more. One day, we'll stand before God, and in that moment, nothing else will matter. The long seasons of waiting will make sense. The hardships will fade away. And we'll realize that the best was never behind us—it was always ahead.

So as much as we anticipate the peak of the season, let's not lose sight of the bigger picture. The greatest reward isn't found in a successful hunt. It's found in the hope we have in Christ. And that, above all else, is worth the wait.

1 M.O.A.
Some things in life are worth the wait, but how we wait makes all the difference. When we trust in what's ahead, waiting shifts from frustration to eager anticipation. Hunters prepare all year for the best days of the season, and as followers of Christ, we are called to live in preparation for something far greater—eternity with Him. Are we setting our sights on what truly lasts, or are we getting caught up in what's temporary?

Mission: Live with an eternal perspective. Shift your focus from temporary rewards to the things that truly last. Just like you prepare for the best days in the woods, prepare your heart daily for the kingdom that's ahead.

Obedience: Invest in what matters most. Spend time in God's Word, deepen your faith, and live in a way that reflects the hope you have in Christ. Make choices that align with eternity rather than just the present moment.

Accuracy: Evaluate how you spend your time and energy. Are you chasing things that will fade, or are you living for something greater? True success is measured by a life that reflects God's purpose, not just temporary achievements.

PRAYER

Dear Jesus, thank You for the promise of eternity with You. In the midst of this life, with all its ups and downs, help me to never lose sight of the incredible future You have prepared. When I grow impatient or distracted by temporary things, remind me that the best is yet to come. Give me a heart that longs for heaven, a mind that stays focused on what truly matters, and a spirit that eagerly anticipates the day I will stand in Your presence. Until then, help me to live faithfully, preparing my heart for eternity and pointing others toward the hope that is found in You. Thank You for the joy of knowing that what awaits is beyond anything I could ever imagine. In Jesus' name, Amen.

DAY 20
THE WEIGHT OF THE MOMENT

VERSE

*I have fought the good fight, I have finished the race,
I have kept the faith.*
2 Timothy 4:7

THE TARGET

Some moments in life carry more weight than others—defining moments that test our character, faith, and resolve. These moments don't give us time to prepare; they reveal who we already are. Paul, nearing the end of his life, looked back with confidence, knowing he had remained faithful despite every challenge. When the pressure is on, how will we respond? Will we stay faithful, obedient, and trust God? Or will fear and uncertainty dictate our decisions?

ZEROED IN

The waiting is finally over. It's the peak of the rut, and your target buck is making his way straight into range. Every calculated plan, every hour spent scouting, and every ounce of preparation has led to this moment. Then suddenly, you feel it—your heart pounds like a war drum, your hands start trembling, and your breath shortens. Buck fever has arrived, and there's no stopping it now.

DAY 20 THE WEIGHT OF THE MOMENT

I'll never forget the first buck I ever shot. It was a defining moment, one that is burned into my memory forever. We had just gotten access to a new farm, and there was a monster buck on the property. The weekend before, we spotted him at 90 yards with six does, and there was no chance he was coming in for a shot. That brief encounter only fueled my anticipation.

The problem was, we got access to the land late in the summer and didn't have time to set up many tree stands. So, I found myself sitting on a bucket at the edge of a ravine, trying to stay as still as possible. That's when I heard it—leaves rustling, hooves pounding against the earth. The unmistakable sound of a chase.

Then, stepping into a clearing at 45 yards, a 7-point buck appeared. My heart rate skyrocketed, and my entire body started shaking. I was only 11 years old, and I had never experienced anything like this before. My hands gripped my bow, but my sights bounced uncontrollably. It felt as if my body was betraying me in the most important moment.

I forced myself to take a deep breath. Then another. The world seemed to narrow, everything else fading away as I locked in on my target. The weight of the moment was unbearable. Then, I squeezed the release. The arrow flew, and in the same instant, I nearly fell off my bucket. My entire body trembled uncontrollably, and the adrenaline rush was unlike anything I had ever felt.

Waiting and trusting that something better is coming goes against everything culture tells us, yet the greatest things in life often require patience and preparation. Still, buck fever has a way of creeping in when I've been locked on a buck just out of range for what feels like forever. Those moments test everything—my patience, my clarity, and my ability to stay locked in.

The weight of every second, when time slows and a buck chases a doe right past my stand, is impossible to ignore. Everything in me screams to act, to take the shot, to not let the moment slip away. But I've learned over the years that staying locked in is everything. In the chaos of a hunt, a single moment—one decision—determines everything.

Pressure has a way of exposing who we really are. It reveals what we've prepared for, but more than that, it shows what we truly believe. In the woods, when that buck finally steps into range, your adrenaline surges, your heart pounds, and for a few seconds, the entire world slows down. The weight of the moment is overwhelming. And in that instant, everything comes down to a single decision.

This isn't just something that happens in hunting. Life is full of moments like this—times when the pressure is immense, when the weight of what's at stake is undeniable. These are the moments where our faith is tested, where our character is revealed. It's one thing to say we trust God, to say we believe He's in control, to say we'll remain faithful no matter what. But when the pressure is on—when temptation is staring us in the face, when our integrity is on the line, when the easier path is right in front of us—will we still hold onto what we say we believe?

Paul understood this reality well. Near the end of his life, he reflected on his journey, knowing he had endured every hardship and remained faithful to his calling. He had stayed on course, never wavering in his devotion to Christ, and now, the finish line was in sight. His confidence didn't come from an easy path, but from the choices he had made in the hardest moments—the times when faith required perseverance, when obedience meant trusting God despite opposition.

Jesus also experienced the weight of the moment like no one else ever has. In the Garden of Gethsemane, on the night before His crucifixion, He knew the suffering ahead, knew the cost, and He wrestled with it. The pressure was so great that He sweat blood, yet He remained unwavering, determined to finish the mission set before Him. Just as Paul later reflected on completing his race, Jesus embraced His purpose fully, demonstrating that true victory is won in the decision to endure, not just in the final outcome. His faithfulness under the most intense pressure set the ultimate example of what it means to finish well.

1 M.O.A.

The weight of the moment isn't something we can avoid. It will come, whether we're ready or not. The real question is how we will respond when it does. Faithfulness under pressure isn't about never feeling the weight—it's about choosing to trust God in it. It's about staying obedient, even when fear, doubt, or uncertainty press in. It's about refusing to take shortcuts, even when compromise would be easier. It's about remaining faithful in the moment, even when everything in us wants to take control. The greatest victories in life aren't found in moments of ease, but in the moments when the pressure is high, and we still choose to trust God and follow Him.

Mission: Respond well in defining moments. When the weight of a moment bears down on you—whether in temptation, trials, or tough decisions—choose faithfulness. The goal isn't avoiding pressure but responding well under it.

Obedience: When faced with a high-pressure moment, pause and surrender it to God. Instead of acting impulsively, pray for wisdom and strength. Prepare yourself now by staying rooted in Scripture, surrounding yourself with godly influences, and committing to obedience before the pressure comes.

Accuracy: Faithfulness under pressure isn't about how often you face it—it's about how you respond. You'll know you're growing when the weight of the moment doesn't shake you but refines you. A strong faith isn't one that never feels the pressure—it's one that chooses to trust God in the middle of it.

PRAYER

Father, I know defining moments will come. In those moments, help me rely on You. Strengthen my faith so I trust You, even when the outcome is uncertain. Just as Paul endured to the end and Jesus embraced His purpose despite the weight of the cross, help me stay faithful. When I'm tempted to take the easy way out, remind me that true victory comes through trusting You. I surrender every moment to You. Teach me to rely on Your strength, and when the pressure comes, let me be found faithful. In Jesus' name, Amen.

DAY 21
ONE STEP AT A TIME (PART 1)

VERSE

Let us not become weary in doing good, for at the proper time we will reap a harvest if we do not give up.
Galatians 6:9

THE TARGET

It's one thing to start strong—it's another thing to keep going when no one's watching, when progress feels slow, and when the outcome isn't clear. That's where faith gets tested. That's where character is built. Not in the big moments, but in the small, steady steps that follow. The kind of faith God honors isn't just about bold beginnings—it's about consistent obedience, even when the payoff feels far away. So when the results don't come right away, will you keep taking one step at a time?

ZEROED IN

There's nothing quite like the moment after the shot. Your adrenaline is pumping, your heart is racing, and for a few seconds, you can't decide whether to celebrate or panic. You replay it in your head—did I rush it? Was the angle good? How did he react? And then reality sets in: the real work just started.

Tracking is one of the most underrated and misunderstood parts of hunting. Everyone loves to talk about the moments leading up to the shot, but not enough people talk about the tracking. It's slow. It's technical. It's often muddy, dark, and full of second-guessing. I've been on tracks that lasted hours. I've crawled through brush on my hands and knees, flashlight in one hand, terrain app in the other, just trying to find one more drop to confirm I'm still on the right path.

Sometimes it's obvious—bright blood, easy trail, deer down within sight. Other times? It's a mess. No exit wound, poor lighting, blood that disappears after 50 yards, and you're stuck wondering whether to grid search, back out, or keep pushing forward.

I remember one particular blood trail that led me through thick timber, down a ravine, across a creek, and back up a steep hillside. For some reason, that deer just wouldn't go down. Every time I thought I was close, I'd find another drop further along—just enough to keep me in the game.

When you're two hours in, soaked in sweat, legs scraped, and crawling through stuff that definitely wasn't cleared for humans, the mental game kicks in hard. You could just give up. Come back later. Call it lost. But if there's one thing tracking has taught me, it's this—you don't give up when you know something's on the line.

That lesson translates way beyond the woods. Galatians 6:9 tells us that we will reap a harvest if we do not give up. It's not about hoping something turns up—it's about continuing in faith when the signs get scarce. It's about trusting that obedience matters, even when you don't see the payoff yet.

Spiritually, we all know how to pull the trigger. We say yes to God, commit to change, take the first step, but what happens after that? What do we do when it's not exciting anymore? When the trail isn't obvious? When faith feels more like work than a mountaintop moment? That's where a lot of people walk away. Not because they didn't believe, but because they didn't expect the in-between to be so hard.

The Bible makes it clear that following Jesus isn't just a moment—it's a walk. A long walk sometimes. 2 Corinthians 5:7

says, "For we walk by faith, not by sight." That verse hits differently when you're 300 yards into a tracking job and the blood trail just disappeared in a sea of oak leaves. Walking by faith doesn't mean you always know where the next step is. It means you keep moving anyway. One drop. One clue. One obedient decision at a time.

The Christian life isn't always filled with obvious signs or spiritual highs. There are seasons where it feels like you're tracking something that doesn't want to be found. You've prayed, obeyed, done your best—and still, the answer hasn't come. The temptation in those moments is to throw up your hands and call it a loss. But that's exactly where the enemy wants you to stop— ten minutes before breakthrough, one step before recovery.

Just like tracking, faithfulness in those moments isn't flashy. It's slow. It's intentional. It's diligent. It's not about being perfect—it's about not quitting when it's hard. Eventually, I found that doe from the long track. She was piled up just past a bush near one of our other stands. And I thought to myself—what if I had given up 30 yards ago?

You don't always get the payoff right away. But the promise in Galatians 6:9 is clear: "At the proper time, we will reap a harvest—if we do not give up." So if you're following God right now and it feels more like a blood trail than a victory lap, don't give up. Keep praying. Keep obeying. Keep looking for the next step, because the harvest might be one step away.

1 M.O.A.

It's not hard to start something with passion. The challenge is staying consistent when progress slows down and motivation fades. Spiritually, that's where many people drift—not because they stopped believing, but because they stopped moving. Faith was never meant to be a one-time decision; it's a daily pursuit. Obedience doesn't always feel exciting, and growth rarely happens overnight. But step by step, day by day, God shapes something lasting in those who refuse to quit.

Mission: Our mission is to remain faithful and persistent, even when the path isn't clear or the results aren't immediate. Just as a hunter stays on the trail despite uncertainty, we are called to trust God and continue walking by faith.

Obedience: Whether you're struggling with doubt or facing challenges, remain steadfast in your commitment. Your perseverance, even in the small things, matters and it will lead to the harvest God has promised. Keep seeking Him in prayer, studying His Word, and walking faithfully through each day.

Accuracy: Evaluate how you respond when progress slows or you encounter setbacks. Are you continuing in obedience, trusting that God is working even when it doesn't feel like it? Or are you tempted to walk away when things get hard? If you feel weary, ask God to strengthen your resolve and keep you on the path, trusting that His timing is perfect, and that the harvest will come when the time is right.

PRAYER

God, I want to be someone who doesn't quit when the trail gets hard to follow. Help me trust You when the path isn't clear and the results don't come quickly. Give me the strength to keep walking, the focus to keep obeying, and the faith to believe You're still at work, even when I can't see it yet. Remind me that one step at a time is enough when I'm following You. Shape my character in the steady steps, and help me hold on to Your promises until the harvest comes. In Jesus' name, Amen.

DAY 22
ONE STEP AT A TIME (PART 2)

VERSE

Brothers and sisters, I do not consider myself yet to have taken hold of it. But one thing I do: Forgetting what is behind and straining toward what is ahead, I press on toward the goal to win the prize for which God has called me heavenward in Christ Jesus.
Philippians 3:13-14

THE TARGET

Paul reminds us that our journey of faith is forward-focused, not bound by past failures or successes. The goal is pressing on toward the prize that God has promised—an eternal life with Him. As we navigate life's challenges, we're called to let go of what lies behind and strive toward what lies ahead, with determination and purpose. This passage challenges us to not get stuck in past mistakes, missed opportunities, or even our past accomplishments. Instead, we are to keep our eyes fixed on Christ, moving forward with the assurance that God is leading us toward something greater. Reflect today on where you may be looking backward, and how you can shift your focus to the prize that awaits you in Christ.

ZEROED IN

Well, you got the deer. That's the high point—the adrenaline rush, the excitement, the feeling of all your hard work finally paying off. But then you realize that the hardest part is yet to come.

The worst is when you're alone. And if you've hunted solo, you know exactly what I mean. As you probably remember, the past few years of hunting for me have been mostly a one-man show. I'm obsessed with the process, don't get me wrong, but I've definitely had moments where I said a quick prayer for strength once I found the deer.

I'll never forget one morning—I shot a big doe, clean shot, perfect moment. But then I realized I had walked nearly half a mile to get into that stand, and this deer decided to crash even farther in the opposite direction, deep into a bottom that might as well have been in a different zip code.

I've had some drags I absolutely dreaded. There's nothing glamorous about pulling a mature deer uphill through thick brush, wet leaves, and mud. I've got a four-wheeler, but some of the places I hunt don't allow them. Other times, it's too thick to get through or just plain inconvenient. So it's the sled. Or worse—the rope drag. You strap it around the antlers or shoulders, lean forward, and start hauling. Every ten steps you're gasping for breath, legs burning, hands blistered. You tell yourself, "Just make it to the next tree... okay, now to that rock..."

And then, finally, after who knows how long, you get back to the truck. But you're not done yet. Now you have to lift it up into the bed. If there's no one else around to help, you do the awkward deadlift-slide-flop maneuver that makes you feel heroic and ridiculous at the same time.

Once it's loaded and strapped down, though, man—it's hard to describe the feeling. You peel off the sweaty layers, slump into the seat, guzzle a water bottle, and just sit there for a minute. Everything hurts, but it's the kind of pain that feels good. You finished the job. You didn't quit when it got heavy. There's something about that walk out—the weight, the effort, the grind—that sticks with you.

That walk out is a powerful picture of what it means to follow Christ.

There's a lot of focus in faith circles about the "moment of decision," the mountaintop experience, the spiritual high, and the breakthrough. Those moments matter, but that's not the whole story. Just like hunting, the shot isn't the end. It's the beginning of the hard part.

The Apostle Paul had every reason to coast. He'd accomplished more than most of us ever will—churches planted, letters written, persecution endured. But near the end of his life, he wrote these words in Philippians 3:13–14: "Forgetting what is behind and straining toward what is ahead, I press on toward the goal..."

Paul didn't drag his faith behind him like a trophy. He carried it forward like a calling. He understood that spiritual success doesn't come from one moment of obedience. It's the cumulative impact of a thousand small choices. It's choosing to keep going when it's inconvenient. When no one is watching. When the weight gets real.

Sometimes, following Jesus feels just like dragging a deer uphill through thick woods. You've done the right thing, made the hard call, obeyed the leading, and now comes the effort. Forgiveness takes work. Faithfulness in marriage takes work. Parenting takes work. So does integrity, discipline, and purity. It's a spiritual grind—and some days, you're tempted to quit. To let go of the rope. To settle for "good enough."

But here's the thing, there's no shortcut to the truck. There's no harvest without the haul.

In the moments when faith feels heavy, when your effort feels unnoticed, when obedience feels exhausting, and when you're not sure if you can keep going, remember this—God sees every step. God isn't after big moments; He's after steady obedience.

Hebrews 12:11 says, "No discipline seems pleasant at the time, but painful. Later on, however, it produces a harvest of righteousness and peace for those who have been trained by it." That verse doesn't promise that the walk out will be easy. But it does promise it'll be worth it.

So if you're dragging right now, if your spiritual legs are burning and your back is sore, don't give up. Don't walk away from the work God gave you just because it's hard. Finish the drag. Lift the weight. Press on. Because one day, you'll sit back—worn out, emptied, and filled with a strange kind of peace—and know that you didn't quit when it mattered. You carried it all the way home.

1 M.O.A.

The walk out after the shot is where your commitment is tested. It's not flashy, and no one's cheering you on. Faith becomes real in the quiet, exhausting, uncomfortable steps that follow obedience. You don't press on because it's easy. You press on because the calling is worth it. The reward isn't just in the moment. It's in finishing what you started.

Mission: Keep moving forward. When the adrenaline fades and the work sets in, stay committed to what God has called you to carry. He hasn't just asked for your "yes"—He's asking for your follow-through.

Obedience: Think about the area of your life where the real weight is being felt, whether it's family, discipline, purity, leadership, or calling. Don't let the heaviness convince you to quit. Ask God for the strength to carry it faithfully.

Accuracy: You'll know you're growing when you stop needing every moment to feel exciting and start trusting that every obedient step, no matter how heavy, is leading you somewhere good.

PRAYER

God, I know that following You doesn't end with a single step. It's a daily walk. There are times when obedience feels heavy, when the path is uphill, and when it would be easier to stop. But I don't want to give up when the work gets hard. Give me strength for the steps ahead. Help me stay faithful in the unseen moments, steady under the weight, and committed to what You've called me to carry. Teach me to trust that You're with me in every part of the walk, not just in the breakthrough, but in the work that follows it. In Jesus' name, Amen.

DAY 23
JUST A MOUNT

VERSE

For all those who exalt themselves will be humbled, and those who humble themselves will be exalted.
Luke 14:11

THE TARGET

There's a big difference between celebrating a win and needing others to know you won. Pride often disguises itself as confidence, achievement, or even thankfulness—but deep down, it's fueled by the desire to elevate ourselves. Jesus flips the script. He doesn't reward the loudest or the flashiest. He honors those who choose humility, even when they have every reason to boast. In the kingdom of God, the highest place doesn't go to those who lift themselves up. It's given to those who know how to stay low. So when success comes, what do you do in the spotlight?

ZEROED IN

There's something special about a good mount on the wall. You know the ones I'm talking about—the kind of deer or fish that stops people in their tracks when they walk into a room. Every hunter and angler has that one they're especially proud of. And to be fair, they should be. That buck didn't just fill out a tag and climb onto the wall by itself.

DAY 23 JUST A MOUNT

Mounts tell a story. They represent hours of scouting, early mornings, weather endured, and lessons learned from mistakes. And sometimes, just sometimes, they represent the moment it all came together.

I've got a few on the wall that bring back some serious memories. They're more than decorations. They're reminders of the pursuit and the reward. They're tied to a specific season in life. Some of them came after a dry spell. Some were surprises. Some were long-awaited goals finally checked off the list.

But none of that compares to what a guy I know has. His wall is covered in saltwater fish—bright-colored mahi, a sailfish with a long sweeping bill, even a mounted shark. It's the kind of setup that makes people stop and stare. You don't have to ask if he's had some big days on the water—it's obvious. That shark alone gets more attention than anything else in the room. I honestly can't blame him for putting it front and center.

We all have those trophies, things we're proud of, moments that make us stand a little taller when they come up. They may not all be on the wall, but they're in our minds and our stories. And that's not wrong. In fact, it's good to remember what you've worked hard for. It's okay to celebrate something God has allowed you to accomplish. The danger is when the trophy starts being more about you than the story it tells.

Pride isn't always loud. It doesn't always show up with a boast or a spotlight. Sometimes, it looks like a subtle shift in the heart—a quiet craving to be noticed, admired, or affirmed. And before you know it, that mount on the wall becomes a mirror. Instead of telling a story about the hunt, the discipline, or God's provision, it tells a story about you. How skilled you are. How patient. How lucky. How deserving. It stops pointing outward and starts pointing inward.

That's the kind of pride Jesus warns against in Luke 14:11: "For all those who exalt themselves will be humbled, and those who humble themselves will be exalted." That's a strong warning. And it cuts a little deeper when you realize He wasn't warning the loudest in the room. He was challenging the ones who thought they were already right with God.

Because the truth is, success always comes with a temptation. When things go right and we succeed, it's easy to forget who really made it happen. We start thinking we earned it. We're owed the credit. When people don't recognize it, we should help them notice. Just like that, the mount on the wall becomes less about God's work and more about our own image.

Here's the thing, though. God's kingdom doesn't work like the world. Out here, the loudest voice gets the attention. The best résumé gets the promotion. The most followers get the platform. But in the kingdom of God? The one who humbles himself gets the seat of honor. That means God lifts up the one who serves in secret, prays with persistence, and obeys without needing applause. The one who resists the urge to make it about themselves, even when they have every reason to boast, is the one God sees.

Let's be real for a minute. What "trophies" are you holding onto right now? Is it your success? Your reputation? Your knowledge? Your leadership? Your discipline? And more importantly, are they still pointing to God... or to you?

God's not against you having things you're proud of. He's not against you pursuing excellence. But He's absolutely opposed to pride taking root in your heart. Because pride doesn't just block your humility; it blocks your ability to receive more from God. He won't fill what's already full of itself. And the more you elevate yourself, the more God has to bring you back down.

But if you choose humility, even when you could boast, even when you're right, even when you've earned the credit, God promises to lift you up. And His reward is better than anything you could put on a wall.

So hang the mount. Tell the story. Celebrate the moment. But make sure the glory goes where it belongs.

1 M.O.A.

You can't walk in humility and carry pride at the same time. The real issue isn't what's on your wall; it's what's in your heart. Pride feeds on attention, comparison, and self-glory. Humility doesn't. It stays quiet, grounded, and focused on something greater. The more you aim to make your life about God's glory, the less room there is for your own. The more you let go of needing to be noticed, the more clearly others will see Christ in you.

Mission: Let your life reflect God's goodness, not your greatness. Just as we celebrate achievements in life, we are called to make sure our success points to God's provision and not our own pride, knowing that true fulfillment comes from exalting Him, not ourselves.

Obedience: Choose one area of your life where you're tempted to seek attention or affirmation. This week, practice humility—serve quietly, give without recognition, or celebrate someone else's win.

Accuracy: Assess the motivation behind your actions and accomplishments. Are you seeking glory for yourself, or are you giving credit where it's due? True humility reflects in how we handle our successes. Examine your heart and ensure that your victories lead others to God, not to your own image.

PRAYER

Father, thank You for the moments of success and the milestones I've been able to celebrate. Every good thing in my life has come from You. Help me never forget that. When I'm tempted to elevate myself, remind me that You've called me to something better, humility, obedience, and a life that reflects Your glory, not mine. Guard my heart from pride. Teach me to recognize it when it creeps in and give me the courage to lay it down. Let every "trophy" in my life point back to Your grace, Your faithfulness, and Your power. Help me walk in humility and let everything I do bring honor to You. In Jesus' name, Amen.

DAY 24
CONSEQUENCES IN THE COMPROMISE

VERSE

*Be on your guard; stand firm in the faith;
be courageous; be strong.*
1 Corinthians 16:13

THE TARGET

There's a difference between being passionate and being prepared. Wanting to stand strong in your faith isn't enough if your defenses are weak or your guard is down. Scripture doesn't just suggest that we stay alert—it commands it. We're called to be watchful, grounded, and courageous, because there's a real enemy who's always looking for a soft spot to strike. A single moment of spiritual carelessness can cost more than we expect. So when the pressure hits, will you be ready, or will your faith misfire?

ZEROED IN

It was the final weekend of muzzleloader season in late December. There were about three inches of fresh snow on the ground, and I was set up in a ground blind just off a main trail. The woods were dead quiet, and everything felt still. Around 9 a.m., two does started working their way toward me, right down the trail and straight into range. At this point in the season, the goal is simple—fill the freezer. I had the perfect setup, and I was just moments away from doing exactly that.

I waited until the lead doe stepped in close, about ten yards, and slowly pulled the trigger. Nothing. Well, not nothing. My muzzleloader made a pathetic little kerplunk sound, the kind that makes your stomach drop instantly. The bullet quite literally fell out of the barrel and hit the snow in front of me. The does froze, lifted their heads, then trotted off like it was no big deal. I just sat there, stunned.

What I didn't realize at the time was that moisture can really sneak into a muzzleloader. Over the past few weekends, I hadn't been emptying or properly maintaining it between hunts. I'd kept the gun loaded, thinking I was saving time.I didn't think twice about it until that moment when it mattered most. Turns out, somewhere between the cold, the humidity, and my carelessness, the powder had absorbed moisture. And when I squeezed the trigger, the ignition failed. I wasn't unarmed. I wasn't inexperienced. I just wasn't ready.

That moment has stuck with me, not because I missed a doe, but because it exposed something deeper. There's a danger in assuming that because we're equipped, we're also prepared. You can look the part and check every box, but if your foundation is soft, the whole structure is one hard moment away from collapsing. You might know the Word. You might show up to church. You might even be leading others. But if your heart isn't being maintained—if there are cracks forming in your character, your thought life, or your discipline—it's only a matter of time before something fails.

1 Corinthians 16:13 says, "Be on your guard; stand firm in the faith; be courageous; be strong." That's not a soft suggestion. It's a call to spiritual alertness. A call to inspect what's going on beneath the surface. Because the truth is, Satan isn't looking to knock you down in the obvious places. He's looking for small compromises. Quiet gaps. Hidden cracks in your armor. And if you don't deal with them, he'll exploit them. Paul reinforces this in 2 Corinthians 2:11, saying, "…in order that Satan might not outwit us. For we are not unaware of his schemes."

But let's be honest, too many of us are unaware. We know the devil's out there, but we forget that his strategy is subtle. He doesn't show up waving red flags. He shows up in spiritual neglect. In unchecked pride. In delayed obedience. In "I'll deal with that later." And just like wet powder in a muzzleloader, those little things don't seem like much until you need your faith to fire, and all you get is a dud.

Maybe that looks like folding under pressure. Maybe it's giving in to temptation you thought you had under control. Maybe it's realizing your passion for God has dried up, and you're just going through the motions. The muzzleloader story reminds me that readiness isn't just about passion—it's about preparation. It's about keeping your heart primed and your spirit sharp. It's checking your spiritual weapons, even when you don't think you'll need them. The enemy doesn't need to destroy you with one big blow. He just needs to keep you careless long enough that when the pressure hits, you crumble from the inside.

So check your powder. Inspect your heart. Ask the hard questions. Is there unaddressed sin I've let linger? Am I neglecting time with God because I feel "too busy"? Have I let my guard down in what I watch, say, or chase after? God doesn't just want us to be passionate—He wants us to be prepared. Because the moment will come. The pressure will hit. And when it does, you don't want to hear a kerplunk. You want your faith to be ready, steady, and locked in.

Stay sharp. Stay ready. Stay grounded. The truth is, the devil rarely attacks head-on. He works through small compromises that feel harmless in the moment.

1 M.O.A.

Failure doesn't always start loud. Sometimes it starts quietly in what you skip, ignore, delay, or assume won't matter. That's how cracks form. And by the time pressure exposes them, it's too late. The enemy doesn't have to overpower you if he can outwait you. All he needs is a weak spot you never dealt with. You're not just standing firm against the world. You're standing guard over your own heart.

Mission: Stay vigilant. Don't just sharpen your knowledge or passion. Pay attention to the places that are starting to corrode. Ask God to expose the subtle compromises before they become costly ones.

Obedience: Choose one area this week to inspect with honesty. Have you been spiritually lazy? Overconfident? Avoiding conviction? Confess it, reset your focus, and take a step toward repair.

Accuracy: You're growing when preparation becomes part of your rhythm—not just your reaction. A strong faith doesn't just show up for the obvious battles. It stays ready, even in the quiet moments of distraction where the real war often begins.

PRAYER

Dear Jesus, help me stay ready. I don't want to look strong and come up empty when it matters. Show me the areas I've been neglecting. Expose the cracks I've ignored. And give me the discipline to fix them before they fail me. I know the enemy is patient, but I also know You're stronger. Train me to be alert. Keep my heart primed and my spirit sharp so I'm not caught off guard. I want to stand firm, stay faithful, and be ready for whatever comes. In Jesus' name, Amen.

POST-SEASON

DAY 25
LOOKING BACK TO MOVE FORWARD

VERSE

I applied my heart to what I observed and learned a lesson from what I saw.
Proverbs 24:32

THE TARGET

Wisdom comes from applying what we've learned, not just from experiencing something. Proverbs 24:32 reminds us that observing the results of what happens, whether good or bad, gives us insight for the future. As we reflect on the season that's passed, we have an opportunity to apply those lessons and approach what's next with greater focus and intention. The real question is whether you will take the time to apply what you've learned or if you'll walk away unchanged.

ZEROED IN

There's something about the end of a hunting season that makes you pause. Whether it was a successful year or one filled with missed opportunities, it's a time to reflect. You think back on the days that went just as planned and the ones that left you scratching your head. You remember the lessons learned when the wind didn't cooperate, when you set up too close or too far, or when that one buck got away because you became impatient.

The same goes for fishing. When summer winds down and the mornings start getting cooler, you look back on the long days on the water. Some days, the fish seemed to jump right onto the hook. Other days, you cast for hours with nothing to show but tired arms and tangled lines. Whether it was a good season or a challenging one, every outing teaches you something if you're willing to pay attention.

Wrapping up a season isn't just about packing up your gear and calling it done. It's about taking the time to ask yourself what worked, what didn't, and what needs to change next time. If you don't learn from the season that's passed, you're bound to repeat the same mistakes in the one that's coming.

There was one season I kept hunting a stand because of all the sign—scrapes, rubs, well-worn trails. On paper, it looked perfect. But the wind was never right when I was there, and I knew it. Still, I convinced myself I could make it work. I hunted it anyway. Deer blew out every time. I wasn't frustrated because I didn't know better—I was frustrated because I ignored what I knew. That's the lesson I almost missed. It wasn't about lack of information—it was about application. I wasn't willing to change my approach. That mindset doesn't just cost you a hunt—it'll cost you growth in your faith too.

Proverbs 24:32 reminds us that wisdom comes from applying what we've observed. King Solomon, known for his God-given wisdom, didn't just glance at a neglected vineyard and move on. As he walked past the field of a lazy man, he saw thorns and weeds overtaking the land and the stone wall crumbling down. But he didn't just observe the condition of the field—he reflected on what he saw and applied the lesson to his own life. The same principle applies to our spiritual lives. God doesn't just want us to go through seasons. He wants us to grow through them.

When life is going well, it's easy to move on without pausing to reflect. And when things don't go the way we hoped, it's tempting to just push past the disappointment and focus on what's next. But just like you can't improve as a hunter or angler without learning from past seasons, you can't grow spiritually without reflecting on where you've been. Taking time to pause and evaluate gives us clarity and wisdom for what lies ahead.

That's exactly what Paul encourages us to do in 2 Corinthians 13:5. He says, "Examine yourselves to see whether you are in the faith; test yourselves. Do you not realize that Christ Jesus is in you—unless, of course, you fail the test?" Paul is clear. Reflection involves taking an honest inventory of where you stand and making adjustments for what's ahead.

In your walk with Christ, are you taking time to reflect? Are you looking back on the seasons you've walked through and asking what God was teaching you? Are you learning from the moments when you trusted Him fully and from the times when you didn't? Are you applying those lessons so that you're more prepared for the next challenge?

Just like a seasoned hunter doesn't ignore the patterns he saw last season, a growing follower of Christ doesn't forget the lessons learned along the way. We take time to evaluate, identifying where we grew, where we stumbled, and where we need to adjust moving forward. And if we don't? We risk walking into the next season with the same blind spots, the same weaknesses, and the same missed opportunities.

The hard truth is that if we're not intentional about learning from the past, we're setting ourselves up for failure in the future. Growth doesn't happen by chance. It happens when we pause, reflect, and apply what God has shown us—the good, the bad, and everything in between.

So don't let this season pass without learning what God wants to show you. Take time to reflect on what He's been teaching you, because what you learn now will shape how you approach the next season.

1 M.O.A.

The best hunters and anglers pay attention to what worked, what didn't, and what needs to change. Spiritual growth works the same way. We can't expect to grow if we move from one season to another without stopping to reflect. Taking time to pause and evaluate gives us the wisdom to face what's ahead with greater focus and intention. Without reflection, we risk stepping into the next season with the same blind spots and missed opportunities.

Mission: Learn from the past season. Take intentional time to reflect on what God has shown you in this season of life. Look back on where you've grown, where you've stumbled, and where He's calling you to make adjustments.

Obedience: Make reflection a habit. Set aside specific time this week to pause and pray. Ask God to show you the areas where He's been working and where He wants to refine you. Write down what you learn and commit to applying those lessons moving forward.

Accuracy: When you apply what you've learned, your choices will reflect the lessons God has taught you. Growth isn't about gaining knowledge—it's about living differently because of what you've seen and experienced.

PRAYER

Lord, I know that growth doesn't happen by accident. Too often, I move on without reflecting on what You've been teaching me. I don't want to miss the lessons You've placed in my path. Give me the discipline to pause, the clarity to see where You're working, and the wisdom to apply those lessons moving forward. Teach me to recognize the patterns in my life that need to change and the areas where You're calling me to grow. Help me approach the next season with a heart that's ready to trust You more and follow You more closely. In Jesus' name, Amen.

DAY 26
THE SOURCE OF IT ALL

VERSE

Every good and perfect gift is from above, coming down from the Father of the heavenly lights, who does not change like shifting shadows.
James 1:17

THE TARGET

It's easy to look at our achievements and assume they're the result of planning, effort, and strategy. James 1:17 reminds us of something deeper. Behind every good outcome, whether in the field or in life, there's a greater source. God is the One who provides the strength, the opportunity, and even the breath in our lungs. When we forget that, we risk believing the blessings we enjoy are earned rather than entrusted. As we reflect on what we've received, we're called to move from self-sufficiency to humility and gratitude, acknowledging that God's provision is constant, even in seasons when it feels like we've done everything ourselves.

ZEROED IN

As you look back on the season, reflecting on moments in the stand, fellowship with friends and family, and quiet walks through the woods, it's important to stop and consider where it all comes from. Whether it's the meat you've put in the freezer or the memories you've stored in your heart, every part of the experience points to a deeper truth. All good things begin with God.

In a culture that celebrates hard work, self-reliance, and grit, it's tempting to believe success is something we earn entirely on our own. And yes, discipline, preparation, and perseverance matter. But Scripture reminds us that behind every result, every reward, is a Provider. James 1:17 says, "Every good and perfect gift is from above, coming down from the Father of heavenly lights." That includes the visible wins, such as filling a tag or finding yourself in the right place at the right time, as well as the unseen blessings like the health to get in the woods, the patience to wait, and the opportunity to pursue what you love.

Hunting is a clear picture of this partnership. We can scout, prepare, and study patterns all season long, but the outcome is never guaranteed. That moment when a deer steps into range isn't just a result of our planning—it's an example of God's provision. He is the One who opens the door. The harvest is His to give, not something we take by effort alone.

This understanding shifts our perspective. It reminds us to approach both success and waiting with humility. The food we enjoy isn't just a product of our work; it's a gift with which we've been entrusted. Even the routine trip to pick up venison from the processor can become a moment to pause and acknowledge that what we have is only possible because of God's generosity.

It also challenges us to examine our hearts. Have we begun to believe that we've earned everything we have? Have we started to rely more on our own effort than on God's grace? These aren't easy questions, but they're necessary. When we start thinking of ourselves as the sole providers, pride begins to take root. Gratitude fades. The glory that belongs to God quietly shifts toward us.

I've noticed this more often in my career than anywhere else. When something goes well or a promotion comes through, it's easy to chalk it up to hard work or talent and forget that God is the One who opened the door. That same mindset can creep in while hunting, too.

I remember opening weekend of bow season one year—I'd picked a spot by a decent-sized creek. My buddies were scattered across the woods, but I went the deepest in. That morning, I saw five bucks and two does. I walked out of the woods feeling like I'd nailed it—like I knew exactly where to be, and when. And while I had put in the work, the truth is, that morning was a gift. God didn't bless me because I chose the right tree. He blessed me because He's good—and He could've shown up no matter where I sat.

The same thing happens when I open the freezer and see it stocked with meat. Yes, I got up early, climbed into the stand, and made the shot, but I didn't put the deer there. God did.

It's all from Him. It always has been.

God absolutely values effort. He designed us to work, to pursue excellence, and to use our skills faithfully. Effort, disconnected from dependence, leads us down a path of spiritual dryness. True growth comes when we bring both our dedication and our dependence into every pursuit. When we offer our work to God and trust Him with the outcome, we cultivate a heart that's not only productive but also full of gratitude.

This perspective isn't just for the woods. It applies to every part of life. Our families, careers, health, relationships, and moments of rest are all touched by God's hand. The same God who provided the deer is the same One who provides strength when we're weary, peace when life is chaotic, and joy in seasons we didn't plan.

Gratitude isn't about ignoring our role or minimizing our effort—it's about recognizing that we don't do any of it alone. God is not a distant observer; He's the One who breathes purpose into our work and fills our days with opportunities to see His goodness.

As you close this season and prepare for whatever comes next, take time to reflect. Not just on the hunts or the highlights, but on the faithfulness of the One who walked with you through it all. Whether you experienced success this year or came up short, the greatest gift is knowing that God never changes, and His provision is constant.

Let your gratitude lead you. Let it shape your heart and habits. Because when we live with the awareness that every good thing comes from above, it transforms not just how we hunt—but how we live.

1 M.O.A.

It's easy to get caught up in the work—whether that's hunting, building a career, or pursuing any goal. But the real challenge comes when we recognize that our efforts are part of something much bigger. God is the source of all our blessings, and we are entrusted with the responsibility to wisely manage what He has given us. The key to lasting growth, success, and fulfillment is recognizing God's hand in it all.

Mission: Stop focusing only on the work and start focusing on where it comes from. Acknowledge God as the source of every good gift, and take time to thank Him for the blessings that often go unnoticed.

Obedience: Reflect on areas where you've become self-reliant or complacent. Ask God to show you where you've failed to recognize His provision, and seek humility in your actions and gratitude in your heart.

Accuracy: A prepared heart doesn't just work hard—it acknowledges the Provider. You'll know you're growing when you can honestly see God's fingerprints on everything you've been given. When you recognize every good thing as coming from Him, you're stepping into a posture of true humility and gratitude.

PRAYER

Father, Thank You for being the source of every blessing in my life. Help me recognize Your hand in all that I have and remind me that everything I receive is a gift from You. Teach me to be a good steward of all You've entrusted to me, and cultivate a heart of gratitude for Your provision. May I live with humility and thankfulness, always acknowledging that You are the Provider of all things. In Jesus' name, Amen.

DAY 27
QUALITY TIME, LASTING IMPACT

VERSE:

Start children off on the way they should go, and even when they are old they will not turn from it.
Proverbs 22:6

THE TARGET

Parenting isn't just about providing; it's about guiding and leading by example. Proverbs 22:6 encourages us to train our children in the right way, not just with words but through the way we live. The most powerful lessons come through shared moments, where our actions speak louder than our words. God calls us to be present in our children's lives, showing them what matters most through our example. Our children watch how we prioritize relationships and handle challenges, shaping their understanding of the world. Are you teaching with both your words and your actions?

ZEROED IN

My dad is truly one of the hardest working men I know. He's up before the sun rises and usually doesn't come inside until after the sun sets. He works Monday through Saturday, taking every Sunday as a day of rest. He's been a farmer my whole life, but not your traditional kind. When I was growing up, he operated a tree farm, supplying trees to the public and working contracts with neighboring cities and developers. Later in life, after moving back to Oregon, he started a hazelnut orchard, ran a tree farm, bought a mushroom farm, and jumped into many other entrepreneurial ventures. The man is the definition of hard work and determination—traits that I've always admired.

When I go out to Oregon to visit, I usually help him work before taking some time to explore or go hunting. One day, while we were at his church, we ran into a friend of his who owned a boat and some crabbing gear. He knew I was staying in town for a week and invited us to go crabbing off the coast of Newport, Oregon. Having never done anything like that before, I was excited to give it a try. We decided to go on a Wednesday, and I managed to convince my dad to take the day off from his usual work in the field.

Wednesday finally arrived, and it was a perfect day—cool and clear with a slight breeze. My dad kept saying, "It's a great day to work," but he had agreed to take the day off and decided instead to make it a great day on the water. We drove out to Newport, launched the boat, and were on the water. Coming from the Midwest, this was an experience I never thought I'd get to have. We started dropping our traps into the ocean, and the work began. By the time we got all the traps in the water, we circled back to the first cage. When we pulled it up, it was loaded with crabs. We worked the line, and within a couple of hours, the three of us had our limit of 12 crabs each.

On our way back into the marina, I wanted a picture with one of the bigger crabs. So, I reached in and grabbed one by the back leg. Standing at the back of the boat, my dad got a perfect shot. But just as he was snapping the photo, that crab leaned up and pinched me—hard. I yelled, shaking my hand to get it off, but it wouldn't let go. Finally, it released and flew five feet over my head, landing back into the water. At that point, our crab count went from 36 to 35.

That day is one I'll never forget. And I don't think my dad will either. If you were to ask him what he was supposed to be doing on that beautiful Wednesday in the field, I'm pretty sure he wouldn't remember. But ask him about our time out on the water, and that's a memory that will stick with both of us forever. It wasn't just about the crabbing—it was about spending time together, doing something we don't usually do, and building a memory that meant more than any task could.

Parenting often feels like a balancing act. Between work, responsibilities, and daily routines, it's easy to get caught up in the cycle of tasks. For many parents, the focus shifts toward providing and keeping everything running smoothly. But in the middle of it all, there's a powerful reminder in the story of my day with my dad—sometimes the most valuable thing we can give our children isn't more effort or instruction. It's simply our time. The unplanned, unexpected moments are often the ones that leave the deepest and most lasting impact.

In Proverbs 22:6, we're reminded to "Start children off on the way they should go," but it's not just about telling them what's right—it's about showing them. Our children learn not just from our words, but from the moments we share with them. Whether it's going crabbing, taking a walk, or having a simple conversation, those shared experiences speak louder than any formal lesson. Through them, they learn how to value relationships, enjoy life beyond the daily grind, and prioritize what truly matters.

That memory stuck with me—not just because it was fun, but because it taught me something about presence. Now that I'm a dad, I think about that day often. I want my kids to feel the same thing I felt—that they matter more than my schedule. That I won't just show up for the big moments, but that I'll be present in the quiet, ordinary ones too. Whether it's tossing a football in the yard, reading before bed, or letting them interrupt my to-do list, I want to model a kind of love that isn't rushed. Years from now, they probably won't remember what I was working on, but they'll remember how I showed up for them.

Jesus modeled this beautifully with His disciples. He didn't just teach with words—He led with presence. He spent meaningful, intentional time with them, showing love, compassion, and care through everyday moments. Relationships aren't built in a rush or a speech; they're formed through connection, patience, and consistency. As parents, we're called to follow His example by investing not only in our children's development, but in their hearts—through both guidance and time together.

Each day brings new opportunities to create memories that will last a lifetime. These moments don't have to be big or elaborate. Often, it's the quiet, consistent acts of love that leave the deepest mark. Are you living the example you want to pass on? What are you teaching through the way you spend your time? As we lead our children, let's invest in their faith as well—training them in the ways of the Lord not just with our words, but with our presence.

> **1 M.O.A.**
>
> The time we give our children today shapes the legacy we leave tomorrow. It's not about crafting perfect moments; it's about showing up consistently, being present, and making space for connection. When we step away from the constant pull of tasks and focus on who we're becoming alongside our children, we teach them what truly matters. Our influence isn't measured by how much we provide but by how well we lead with love, humility, and presence. The quiet, intentional moments often become the loudest echoes in their hearts.
>
> **Mission:** Be intentional with your time and presence. Your children won't remember every task you completed, but they will remember how available and engaged you were. Make it a priority to build meaningful connections through shared experiences that reflect God's love and character.
>
> **Obedience:** Set aside time this week to be fully present with your child or children. Put away distractions, say yes to something spontaneous, or plan a simple moment together. Use that time not just for fun, but as an opportunity to listen, encourage, and reflect Christ through your presence.
>
> **Accuracy:** True growth happens when your calendar begins to reflect your values. Look at how you spend your time. Are you prioritizing your relationship with your children in ways that lead them closer to Jesus? Presence over performance leaves a lasting impact.

PRAYER

Lord, thank You for the gift of my children and the precious moments we share together. Help me to be intentional with my time, stepping away from the demands of life to invest in the relationships that matter most. Teach me to prioritize quality time with my children, showing them the love, guidance, and presence they need. Let my actions speak louder than my words, and may I be a reflection of Your love and care in everything I do. Help me recognize the importance of these moments and the impact they will have on their lives. In Jesus' name, Amen.

DAY 28
A SHED OF EVIDENCE

VERSE

For since the creation of the world God's invisible qualities—his eternal power and divine nature—have been clearly seen, being understood from what has been made, so that people are without excuse.
Romans 1:20

THE TARGET

God's presence is all around us, visible in the world He created. Romans 1:20 tells us that God's invisible qualities, His power and divine nature, are made known through the natural world. From the smallest details to the most majestic landscapes, the evidence of God's work is right in front of us. In much the same way, the traces of biblical history are scattered throughout our daily lives, if only we take the time to look. Sometimes, we need to pause and seek out those reminders of God's eternal power—whether in nature, history, or even the stories and teachings passed down through generations. When we open our eyes to see, the evidence of God's creation and presence is all around us, waiting to be noticed.

ZEROED IN

During the offseason, we outdoorsmen are always looking for ways to spend time in the woods. For many of us, shed hunting becomes a prime activity. I had access to a small, isolated patch of woods, about 20 acres, surrounded by agricultural fields. We mostly used those woods for squirrel hunting in the late summer, and I don't ever remember seeing any deer while we were out there. Sure, we'd see tracks from time to time, but we always assumed the deer were just passing through and didn't really call this place home.

One day, during the offseason, I decided to take a walk through that same patch of woods. As I made my way through the woods, something caught my eye. Just off the trail, I noticed something tucked into the brush. It was a massive shed, bigger than anything I'd ever seen in person. It stopped me in my tracks. I can't emphasize enough just how big this shed was. It had incredible mass, points, and kickers. To this day, it's still the largest shed any of us in my family has ever found.

I picked it up and couldn't believe what I was holding. How could a deer like this have been roaming through this small patch of woods, Especially when we'd always assumed it was just a spot for smaller game. It felt like a secret we had missed for years. This wasn't just a random find; it was a reminder that the world around us holds more than meets the eye.

That shed has become a conversation starter every time someone spots it. I never would've guessed I'd find something like that in the same woods we used for squirrel hunting. It was humbling and served as a clear reminder that the most extraordinary things often show up where we least expect them. That moment challenged me to pay closer attention, to stop assuming I've seen it all, and to stay open to wonder in everyday places.

Sometimes, we're so familiar with our surroundings that we stop expecting anything new from them. We walk the same trails, pass the same trees, and assume we know what's out there. That's how it was with those woods where I found the shed. I thought I had seen all there was to see. But one moment changed that and reminded me that God often hides wonder right in the middle of the ordinary.

Romans 1:20 makes it clear that God has left His fingerprints all over creation. His invisible qualities, His power and His divine nature, aren't distant or hidden away. They're woven into the world around us. Whether it's a sunrise that takes your breath away, the quiet beauty of a still forest, or the intricate design of a single leaf, all of it points to a Creator who is not only real but present. We just have to be willing to see it.

The shed I found that day wasn't just a trophy. It was a reminder. It was a reminder that I had underestimated what was right in front of me and, in doing so, nearly missed something incredible. That applies to far more than deer. How often do we walk past evidence of God's goodness, presence, and truth without even noticing? How many moments do we rush through, blind to the sacred hidden within the simple?

God speaks through creation. He teaches us through stillness, through surprise, through unexpected discoveries on quiet trails. But we can't hear Him if we never slow down, if we never take time to look closer. The natural world isn't just scenery—it's a sermon. Every detail, every corner of creation declares the glory of God, if we're willing to listen.

So take a walk. Sit in silence. Study the design of what's around you. The woods, the water, the wind in the trees are not random. It's all part of something intentional, pointing us back to a God who is constantly revealing Himself. Just like that shed antler tucked into the brush, God's presence is often right in front of us. Are we paying attention?

When we begin to look at the world with that perspective, it changes us. We move from assumption to awe, from routine to reverence. Those moments bring us face-to-face with the Creator—not only in church or through Scripture, but out in the woods, across open fields, and woven into the everyday.

1 M.O.A.

God isn't hiding; He is revealing. Every corner of creation is a reflection of His character, His power, and His presence. But we often miss it because we're not looking. The smallest details in nature can become some of the clearest declarations of God's glory when we learn to slow down and pay attention. Just like that unexpected shed in the woods, reminders of God's nearness are often tucked into the places we overlook. When we take time to truly see what's around us, we begin to realize that God is always speaking. We just need to tune in.

Mission: Be intentional about noticing God in your surroundings. Whether you're in the woods, driving to work, or spending time with family, keep your eyes open for the ways He reveals Himself. Creation is more than a backdrop. It's a living testimony to God's power and presence.

Obedience: Set aside time this week to be still and observant in nature. Take a walk, sit in silence, or reflect outdoors. Ask God to open your eyes to the beauty He's placed around you. Let that time deepen your awareness of His nearness.

Accuracy: You are growing when curiosity begins to replace assumptions in your daily life. If you find yourself slowing down more often to notice the details, whether in a leaf, a conversation, or a quiet moment, you are learning to see the world the way God intended—full of wonder and truth.

PRAYER

Dear Jesus, thank You for the beauty You've placed all around me. Too often I rush through life and miss the signs of Your presence right in front of me. Help me slow down. Open my eyes to see You in the details in nature, in quiet moments, and in the simple things I tend to overlook. Teach me to approach each day with curiosity and gratitude, knowing that You are always near. Let the world You created stir something deeper in my heart and draw me closer to You. May I never take Your presence for granted. In Jesus' name, Amen.

DAY 29
PASSING IT ON

VERSE

And the things you have heard me say in the presence of many witnesses entrust to reliable people who will also be qualified to teach others.
2 Timothy 2:2

THE TARGET

Just as Paul instructed Timothy to entrust what he had learned to others, we are called to share our experiences and wisdom with those who are eager to learn. Teaching others is an opportunity to invest in their journey, build relationships, and create lasting memories. As we help someone new to hunting, we are not only imparting knowledge but also helping them build a foundation that will last for years to come.

ZEROED IN

There's something incredibly fulfilling about introducing someone to the world of hunting or fishing. It's not just about showing them how to hunt or fish; it's about giving them a chance to experience the same connection to the outdoors that has brought me so much joy.

I've always been intentional about inviting others into this experience. I remember one time when I invited my old neighbor to join me in a two-man stand. He was brand-new to hunting, and on the way there, I walked him through everything—where deer usually come from, when to move, how to shoulder the gun, and where to aim. As the morning faded, a couple of deer stepped into view. I had a brand-new shotgun in hand, but instead of taking the shot, I handed it to him. As he shouldered the gun, I whispered the yardage and coached him on where to hold the sights. He squeezed the trigger and made a clean shot on his first deer. I'll never forget the look on his face. His excitement was contagious, and in that moment, I felt like I had taken the shot myself. That one moment of success, built on a foundation of trust and shared knowledge, meant more than if I'd filled the tag myself.

Another time, my brother-in-law joined me for a hunt. He had some basic experience, but I still found myself walking him through the nuances—playing the wind, moving quietly, and paying attention to details. The whole way to the woods, I coached him through what to look for and how to think like a hunter. What surprised me, though, was how quickly he picked things up. That morning, he spotted several deer long before I did. He had an ability to scan the woods with such focus. Watching him sharpen that skill over time reminded me that growth happens when someone has the right encouragement and room to develop their instincts.

I grew up with a mentor—someone who taught me the fundamentals, helped me read the rhythms of the outdoors, and laid the groundwork for how I hunt and think today. We spent countless hours in the woods, and whether he realized it or not, those moments shaped me. They gave me a foundation I didn't fully recognize at the time. But looking back, his influence showed me just how valuable it is to pass on what you've learned. It made me want to be the kind of person who shows up, shares what I know, and walks alongside others—just like someone once did for me.

Introducing someone to the outdoors, whether it's hunting, fishing, or simply spending time in the woods, is about more than just sharing a hobby. It's about giving them the opportunity to experience the same joy, discipline, and connection to creation that has shaped you. You're not just teaching them to track a deer or cast a line; you're giving them a gift that has the potential to change how they see the world. And when they step into that experience, something remarkable happens—they grow, gain confidence, and often, they begin to pass that knowledge on to others.

In many ways, this is exactly how spiritual mentorship works. Paul captured this idea perfectly in 2 Timothy 2:2, "And the things you have heard me say in the presence of many witnesses entrust to reliable people who will also be qualified to teach others." Paul's words emphasize the power of multiplication. He wasn't just instructing Timothy to be a good student—he was charging him to pass down everything he had learned, so that those lessons would continue to spread. True discipleship isn't just about transferring knowledge; it's about creating a ripple effect where the truth of God's Word impacts generation after generation.

Mentoring someone, whether in practical skills or in faith, goes beyond simply improving their abilities. It's about investing in who they are becoming. We're giving them the tools to navigate life with perseverance, patience, and trust in God. Just like guiding someone through the woods on their first hunt, walking with someone through a season of life helps them develop the confidence and character they need to succeed—not just in the moment, but for years to come.

Think back to the people who have invested in you. Maybe it was a parent, a mentor, or even a friend who took the time to teach, encourage, and equip you. Their influence likely shaped how you approach life today. Now, consider who God is calling you to invest in. Who in your life needs the encouragement, wisdom, and guidance that you've been blessed to receive?

Mentoring someone doesn't require you to have all the answers. It simply requires a willingness to show up, walk alongside them, and be present in their journey. Just as a good hunting guide doesn't guarantee a successful hunt, a good mentor doesn't promise a trouble-free life. But both equip others to be ready when the moment comes—to face challenges with confidence, faith, and resilience.

But the true beauty of mentorship is that it doesn't stop with one person. When we intentionally pour into someone's life, we're planting seeds that can bear fruit for generations. The person you invest in today may go on to mentor someone else tomorrow, creating a legacy that stretches far beyond what you can see. What happens in the moment matters, but the real impact comes through the faith, wisdom, and knowledge we pass on for the future.

We should find just as much joy in passing on the lessons of life and faith. Trust that God will use these moments to shape both you and those you mentor, creating a ripple effect that extends far beyond anything you could imagine.

> **1 M.O.A.**
> True impact isn't measured by what we accomplish alone but by what continues after us. When we invest in others—whether by sharing skills, offering guidance, or walking alongside them in faith—we equip them to do the same for someone else. The goal isn't just to mentor but to inspire a cycle where what we've poured out continues to ripple outward, creating a lasting legacy.
>
> **Mission:** To intentionally invest time, wisdom, and care into someone else—whether in hunting, faith, or life—with the goal of equipping them not just to succeed, but to confidently pass that knowledge on to others.
>
> **Obedience:** Commit to mentoring someone. Whether you're teaching them the ins and outs of hunting or fishing, or walking with them through a challenging season of life, let your actions reflect Christ. Be present, encourage them, and model what it looks like to lead with grace, patience, and purpose. In doing so, you're not just passing on skills; you're pointing them to the One who shapes every part of life.
>
> **Accuracy:** Measure success not by how much knowledge you pass on, but by how clearly others begin to reflect Christ and lead others toward Him. True impact is found in the ripple effect—when your investment in one life multiplies into many, all pointing back to Jesus.

PRAYER

Dear Jesus, thank You for the people who have invested in me and helped me grow in my faith and in life. Give me the wisdom and patience to pour into others with the same grace and love. Help me to see beyond the immediate and trust that my efforts will multiply in ways I may never witness. Guide me to those who need encouragement, and give me the courage to equip them to lead others. May the impact of my obedience extend far beyond my own reach, leaving a legacy that honors You. In Jesus' name, Amen.

DAY 30
ROOTED IN GRATITUDE

VERSE

Give thanks in all circumstances; for this is God's will for you in Christ Jesus.
1 Thessalonians 5:18

THE TARGET

1 Thessalonians 5:18 teaches us that gratitude is not dependent on our circumstances but is a response to God's constant goodness. Giving thanks in all situations, whether joyful or challenging, is an act of trust that acknowledges God's presence and sovereignty. When we cultivate a heart of gratitude, we align ourselves with God's will, recognizing that He is working in every situation for our good and His glory. This verse challenges us to shift our focus from what we lack to what we've been given, building a foundation of faith and contentment in all aspects of life.

ZEROED IN

If you're anything like me, you grew up watching the guys on TV—the ones with the best gear, perfectly managed hunting land, and top-of-the-line equipment. From expansive properties to box blinds that look like luxury cabins, it's easy to compare what we have to what they show us. Don't get me wrong—I respect those guys. They're skilled, knowledgeable, and we can learn a lot from them.

For most of us, that kind of setup isn't reality. I'm part of a group that takes the resourceful route. We piece together stands from clearance racks, old ladders, and scrap metal—whatever gets the job done. And the truth is, we still walk away with great stories, strong bonds, and memories we'll never forget. You don't need high-end gear to have a meaningful experience in the woods.

It's the same with fishing. Some of my friends have boats and head out every weekend. I don't have one, but casting from the bank still fills me with the same peace. Whether you're in a stand or standing by the water, it's not about the setup—it's about the connection, the people, and the moments that stick.

A few years ago, I lost access to my main hunting property when the landowner sold it. I had hunted that land for years. I knew every ridge, every trail, and every pattern the deer followed. Losing it felt like losing a part of my rhythm—and honestly, I was devastated. At the time, it felt like a major setback. Looking back, I can see how God used that loss to open new doors. It pushed me to build new connections, explore unfamiliar ground, and form relationships that I now cherish. What felt like a closed door eventually became a blessing I didn't expect. I wasn't thankful for the loss, but I learned to be thankful in it—and that's made all the difference.

It's easy to fall into the trap of thinking we need more to enjoy life. The latest gear, the biggest property, the best equipment—all of it looks appealing. When we focus on what we don't have, we risk overlooking the blessings already right in front of us.

1 Thessalonians 5:18 reminds us to "give thanks in all circumstances, for this is God's will for you in Christ Jesus." It doesn't say to give thanks for every circumstance, but in them. That small shift in wording carries a powerful truth. We can recognize God's goodness even when things don't go exactly how we hoped.

A grateful heart changes how we see the world. That old bow becomes more than a tool. It becomes a symbol of memories, growth, and God's provision. The hand-me-down stand isn't just patched together equipment; it's part of the reason we get to spend time with our kids, brothers, or friends. And standing on the bank instead of on a boat might just give us the stillness we didn't know we needed.

Gratitude reorients us. It pulls our attention away from what we lack and helps us focus on the richness of what we already have. Contentment starts when we recognize that God's blessings aren't always flashy or new. They're often simple, steady, and deeply meaningful.

Think about the people you've known who embody that kind of contentment. They don't chase the next best thing. They're fully present, fully thankful. Their peace doesn't depend on possessions. It's rooted in a deep trust in God's goodness. That's the kind of life we're invited to live.

So how do we start? It begins with perspective. We learn to shift our focus from what's missing to what's already in place. We make the choice to recognize the good, even if it's quiet or small. And we give thanks—not just when everything is perfect, but especially when it's not.

When we live like that, we honor God. We draw closer to Him. And we discover a joy that doesn't fade with trends or gear or circumstance. We discover that gratitude isn't just a response to blessings. It is a pathway to a fuller life.

1 M.O.A.
When we stop measuring our lives by what we don't have and start noticing what God has already provided, everything shifts. The old bow, the borrowed stand, the quiet cast from the bank—they become reminders of God's faithfulness, not shortcomings. A grateful heart doesn't need perfect conditions to experience peace and joy. It just needs to pay attention. When we live with thankfulness, we stop chasing the next thing and start cherishing what's already in our hands.

Mission: True gratitude grows when we intentionally shift our focus from what we desire to what we've been given. Our goal is to develop a heart that recognizes and appreciates God's blessings, no matter the circumstances.

Obedience: Pause today and reflect on the blessings that often go unnoticed. Consider the gear that's served you well, the moments in nature that have brought you peace, and the relationships that have enriched your life. Ask God to open your eyes to the good things around you and to help you cultivate a heart that chooses gratitude.

Accuracy: Measure success not by how much you acquire but by how often you pause to acknowledge and thank God for what you already have. A heart that regularly gives thanks is a heart that stays aligned with God's will.

PRAYER

Father, thank You for the countless blessings You've placed in my life. Help me to see beyond what I don't have and recognize the abundance of gifts You've already given me. Teach me to cultivate a heart that gives thanks in all circumstances, whether in seasons of plenty or moments of waiting. Guard my heart against comparison and discontentment, and remind me that true contentment is found not in having more, but in trusting You completely. In Jesus' name, Amen.

DAY 31
A LEGACY THAT LASTS

VERSE

We will not hide them from their descendants; we will tell the next generation the praiseworthy deeds of the Lord, His power, and the wonders He has done.
Psalm 78:4

THE TARGET

Leaving a legacy of faith means more than passing down knowledge; it involves sharing the stories of God's power and the wonders He has worked in our lives. When we tell others about how we've seen God's faithfulness, we plant seeds that can grow long after we're gone. Whether through our words, our actions, or the way we live out our faith daily, we are constantly shaping the spiritual foundation of those who come after us. Psalm 78:4 reminds us that experiencing God's goodness isn't meant to stop with us. We are called to make His mighty works known to those who come after us.

ZEROED IN

When we think about leaving a legacy, our minds often go to tangible things—property, money, or family heirlooms. While those items can hold value and memories, they're temporary. The legacy that matters most is the one that endures beyond this life, the kind rooted in lasting faith. Psalm 78:4 captures this truth with clarity and conviction.

That truth hit me more personally than ever the first time I took my oldest fishing a few weeks ago. We stood at the water's edge, poles in hand, and I realized this moment wasn't just about teaching her to cast. It was about the conversations we'd have, the patience we'd build, and the trust we'd form. That day reminded me that a legacy starts small—in shared time, quiet moments, and the example I set when no one's watching.

Psalm 78:4 pushes us to think beyond ourselves. It urges us to consider the impact our lives will have on generations to come, and to share the stories of God's goodness so His truth carries forward. Just as we pass down outdoor skills or family traditions, we're also given the responsibility to pass down the truth of who God is and what He has done.

That kind of influence isn't built on words alone. It's not about reciting Bible verses or telling someone to go to church. It's about living in a way that reflects the reality of our faith. People need to see trust in action—patience during difficulty, grace when it's not easy, and confidence in God when the path ahead is unclear.

Joshua 24:15 offers a powerful example of that kind of commitment with the words, "But as for me and my house, we will serve the Lord." This wasn't just a personal choice. Joshua made a public declaration that his entire household would follow God. His leadership started at home, just like ours should. Our children and those around us are always watching how we handle pressure, how we spend our time, how we speak about others. It's in these daily choices that they begin to understand what genuine faith looks like.

When I think about what I'm leaving behind, I want my kids to remember more than the hunts or fish. I want them to remember that I turned to prayer when things were uncertain, that I treated others with grace, and that I chose to trust God even when life was hard. That's not a one-time lesson—it's something they pick up over time, in everyday moments.

That being said, we can't leave a legacy from a distance. Meaningful influence starts with showing up. If we're too distracted, too overcommitted, or too distant, we miss the moments that shape hearts. The most powerful lessons often come in the most ordinary settings—like the dinner table, working side by side on a project, or sitting in silence out in the woods. These are the times when trust is built and conversations about faith happen naturally.

Choosing to live with intention doesn't just affect us—it creates a spiritual path for those who follow. Our everyday faith, especially in how we respond to both challenges and victories, becomes a reference point for those watching. It's in that consistency that others begin to see faith as something lived, not just believed.

Our stories matter, too. Sharing how God has shown up in our own lives—whether by providing, protecting, comforting, or convicting—becomes a living testimony. These moments turn abstract faith into something real and relatable. They help others see that God is not distant or detached, but actively present and personally involved in our lives.

I want my kids to grow up knowing God isn't just someone we talk about on Sundays—He's someone we walk with every day. That's the kind of legacy I hope to leave.

> **1 M.O.A.**
> Your legacy isn't built in a single moment; it's shaped in the everyday choices you make to follow Jesus with consistency and love. The way you lead your family, handle adversity, and prioritize what matters most leaves a lasting impression on those who follow you. When your life reflects trust in God through both triumph and trial, you create a blueprint for faith that others can walk in long after you're gone. Legacy begins now in your actions, your example, and the time you invest in others.
>
> **Mission:** Live each day with the awareness that your actions are shaping the spiritual foundation for those who follow you. Make intentional choices that reflect your commitment to Christ,

not just for your own growth but to leave behind a legacy that points others toward Him.

Obedience: This week, look for one opportunity to invest spiritually in someone in your family or circle of influence. That might mean having a conversation about your faith, praying together, sharing a personal story of God's faithfulness, or simply being present in a way that reflects Christ's love.

Accuracy: You're growing when your daily life speaks louder than your words. If others can look at how you live, including how you serve, forgive, and trust God, and walk away with a clearer picture of His character, then you're leaving a legacy that truly matters.

PRAYER

Heavenly Father, thank You for the opportunity to influence the next generation. Help me to live each day with purpose and clarity, knowing that my choices shape more than just my own life. Give me the wisdom to lead with grace, the courage to stand firm in faith, and the humility to point others toward You. Teach me to value the small moments, to be present with the people You've placed in my life, and to share stories of Your goodness with honesty and boldness. May my life reflect Your love in a way that leaves a lasting impact. In Jesus' name, Amen.

EPILOGUE

BUILT TO LAST

The seasons will change. The woods will grow quiet, then loud again. Opportunities will come and go. And through it all, the call remains the same—stay faithful.

This journey isn't about perfection. It's about perseverance. It's about showing up day after day, rooted in truth, grounded in grace, and confident in the One who walks with you. That's why Ephesians 6 reminds us to put on the full armor of God—not just once, but daily. We need truth to steady us. Righteousness to protect us. Peace to guide us. Faith to shield us. Salvation to remind us who we are. And the Word of God to keep us sharp.

Spiritual battles don't always look like battles. Sometimes they look like distractions, discouragement, or doubt. Sometimes, they sound like silence when you're waiting for direction. Or restlessness when God says "wait."

Whether you're in a season of harvest or a season of waiting, be prepared. Stand firm. Trust that even when you don't see the movement, God is still at work.

So keep showing up. Keep trusting. Keep putting on the armor and stepping into each day with boldness, not because it's easy—but because God goes before you, walks beside you, and fights for you.

The legacy you leave won't be built in a single moment, but in the faithful ones—day after day, season after season, step by step.

ACKNOWLEDGMENTS

To my wife, thank you for believing in this project from the very beginning and for giving me the space to run with it. You never once made me feel like this was a burden to our schedule or home life. I love you and am so thankful for your support and encouragement.

To my kids, thank you for always making me smile and reminding me of what truly matters. Every time I left for the woods or spent long hours tucked away in the office, it was you I missed most. I hope this devotional speaks to your hearts someday too.

To my friends, mentors, and hunting buddies who helped shape so many of the stories told here, thank you for the laughs, the lessons, and the memories. I am better for having you in my life.

To the landowners who have generously opened up their property to me over the years, thank you. Your kindness and trust have given me a place to learn, reflect, and grow both as a hunter and in my walk with God.

To my editors and reviewers, thank you for pushing me to dig deeper, stay true to my voice, and refine the message without losing its heart. This book is stronger because of your insight and guidance.

And finally, to every reader who picked up this devotional and spent time in these pages, thank you. My prayer is that you were encouraged, challenged, and reminded that your walk with Christ matters deeply — both in the stillness and in the pursuit.

CREDITS

All Scripture quotations are taken from the Holy Bible, New International Version®, NIV®. Copyright ©1973, 1978, 1984, 2011 by Biblica, Inc.™ Used by permission. All rights reserved worldwide.

Cover design by KnoWhere Outdoors
Cover imagery includes licensed elements from
Shutterstock, used with permission
Interior layout by HMDPublishing.com & KnoWhere Outdoors

STAY IN TOUCH

Thank you for spending time with this devotional—I hope it encouraged you in both your faith and your love for the outdoors. If you'd like to stay connected, follow along for future content, resources, and community stories. I'd love to hear how this journey has impacted you and what God's been teaching you along the way.

Website: www.KnoWhereOutdoors.com

Instagram: @KnoWhereOutdoors

Let's keep the conversation going.

www.ingramcontent.com/pod-product-compliance
Lightning Source LLC
Chambersburg PA
CBHW070631030426
42337CB00020B/3979